First World War
and Army of Occupation
War Diary
France, Belgium and Germany

66 DIVISION
199 Infantry Brigade
204 Machine Gun Company
16 March 1917 - 28 February 1918

WO95/3145/7

The Naval & Military Press Ltd
www.nmarchive.com
Published in association with The National Archives

Published by

The Naval & Military Press Ltd

Unit 10 Ridgewood Industrial Park,
Uckfield, East Sussex,
TN22 5QE England
Tel: +44 (0) 1825 749494

www.naval-military-press.com

www.nmarchive.com

This diary has been reprinted in facsimile from the original. Any imperfections are inevitably reproduced and the quality may fall short of modern type and cartographic standards.

© **Crown Copyright**
Images reproduced by permission of The National Archives, London, England, 2015.

Contents

Document type	Place/Title	Date From	Date To
Heading	WO95/3145/7 204 Machine Gun Company		
Heading	66th Division 199th Infy Bde 204th Machine Gun Coy. Mar 1917-Feb 1918		
Heading	War Diary of 204th Machine Gun Company From 16th March To 31st March 1917		
Miscellaneous	To OC No 20 MG Corps	22/03/1917	22/03/1917
Miscellaneous	Ob 204th G. L.	26/03/1917	26/03/1917
War Diary	Le Harve	16/03/1917	16/03/1917
War Diary	No.2 Rest Camp Le Havre	17/03/1917	18/03/1917
War Diary	Bunny	19/03/1917	20/03/1917
War Diary	Annequin	21/03/1917	31/03/1917
Miscellaneous	Casualty Returns		
Miscellaneous	To D.A.G. 3rd Echelon G.H.Q.		
Heading	War Diary of 204 Machine Gun Company From April 1st To April 30th 1917		
War Diary	Noyelles	01/04/1917	30/04/1917
Miscellaneous	204 Machine Gun Company Special Order	24/04/1917	24/04/1917
Heading	War Diary of 204 Machine Gun Company From May 1st To May 31st 1917		
War Diary	Noyelles	01/05/1917	31/05/1917
Miscellaneous	To D.A.G. 3rd Echelon	02/07/1917	02/07/1917
Heading	War Diary of 204 Machine Gun Compy From 1st June 1917 To 30 June 1917		
War Diary	Noyelles	01/06/1917	20/06/1917
War Diary	Marles Lez Mines	21/06/1917	24/06/1917
War Diary	St. Pol Sur Mer	25/06/1917	30/06/1917
Miscellaneous	Special Relief Order By Captain R.B. Buchanan Commanding 20th Machine Gun Company		
Miscellaneous	To H.Q. 199th Infy Bde		
Heading	War Diary of 204 Machine Gun Company From 1st July 1917 To 31st July 1917		
War Diary	St. Pol Sur Mer	01/07/1917	11/07/1917
War Diary	Ghyvelde	12/07/1917	14/07/1917
War Diary	Coxyde Bains	15/07/1917	31/07/1917
Miscellaneous	Programme of work	14/07/1917	14/07/1917
Miscellaneous	Machine Gun Fire Table		
Heading	War Diary of 204 Machine Gun Coy From 1st August 1917 To 31st August 1917 Vol VI		
War Diary	Coxyde Bains	01/08/1917	31/08/1917
Miscellaneous	Relief Order by Capt. R.E. Buchanan Commanding No.204 M.G. Coy. Appendix II		
Miscellaneous	Programme of work	24/08/1917	24/08/1917
Miscellaneous	Relief Order		
Heading	War Diary of 204 Machine Gun Company From 1st Sept 1917 To 30th Sept 1917 Vol VIII		
War Diary	Coxyde Bains	01/09/1917	11/09/1917
War Diary	Coy H.Q. Coxyde Bains	12/09/1917	12/09/1917
War Diary	Ady. Coy. H.Q. Nieuport Bains	13/09/1917	20/09/1917
War Diary	Coy H.Q. Coxyde Bains	21/09/1917	21/09/1917
War Diary	Ady H.Q. Nieuport Bains	22/09/1917	27/09/1917

Type	Title	From	To
War Diary	Campagne (Ref Map Hazebrouk 5)	28/09/1917	30/09/1917
Miscellaneous	Operation Order Appendix I		
Miscellaneous	Special Relief Order No. 51		
Miscellaneous	Special Relief Order No. 52		
Miscellaneous	204th M.G. Coy		
Miscellaneous	Casualty List		
Miscellaneous	204 Machine Gun Coy.		
Heading	War Diary of 204 Machine Gun Company From 1st Oct To 31st Oct 1917 Vol. VIII		
War Diary	Campagne	01/10/1917	06/10/1917
War Diary	Ypres	06/10/1917	11/10/1917
War Diary	Brandhoek	12/10/1917	13/10/1917
War Diary	Arques	14/10/1917	25/10/1917
War Diary	Malhove Arques	26/10/1917	31/10/1917
Miscellaneous	199 Bde Order No. 60		
Miscellaneous	Report On Operation	09/10/1917	09/10/1917
Miscellaneous	Reinforcements		
Miscellaneous	Casualties 1st Oct 1917 to 31st Oct 1917		
Heading	War Diary of 204 Machine Gun Company From 1st Nov.1917 To 30th Nov. 1917 Vol. IX		
War Diary	Staples	01/11/1917	08/11/1917
War Diary	Westoutre	09/11/1917	09/11/1917
War Diary	Swan Area Ypres	10/11/1917	23/11/1917
War Diary	Berthen Area	24/11/1917	25/11/1917
War Diary	Staples (Sub Area)	26/11/1917	30/11/1917
Miscellaneous	Casualty Return		
Heading	War Diary of 204 Machine Gun Company From 1st Dec' 1917 To 31st Dec' 1917 Vol X		
War Diary	St. Sylvestre Cappel	01/12/1917	31/12/1917
Miscellaneous	Appendix		
Miscellaneous	Programme Of Work	10/12/1917	10/12/1917
Heading	War Diary Of 204 Machine Gun Company 1st Jan 1918 To 31st Jan 1918 Vol XI		
War Diary	St. Sylvestre Cappel	01/01/1918	31/01/1918
Miscellaneous	Movement Relief Order		
Operation(al) Order(s)	204 M.G. Coy. Movement Order No. 1	09/10/1917	09/10/1917
Miscellaneous	Operation Order By Capt R.B. Buchanan Cmdg 204 M.G. Coy	12/01/1918	12/01/1918
Miscellaneous	204 Machine Gun Coy	18/01/1918	18/01/1918
Miscellaneous	204 Machine Gun Coy	24/01/1918	24/01/1918
Miscellaneous	204 Machine Gun Company	30/01/1918	30/01/1918
Heading	War Diary of 204 Machine Gun Company From 1st Feb 1918 To 28th Feb 1918 Vol XII		
War Diary	Canal Area H24a.05.90.	01/02/1918	28/02/1918
Miscellaneous	Appendix		
Miscellaneous	204 Machine Gun Coy - Relief Orders Copy 6		
Miscellaneous	204 Machine Gun Coy - Relief Orders Copy 4		
Miscellaneous	204 Machine Gun Coy - Relief Orders Copy 6		
Miscellaneous	204 Machine Gun Company Copy No. 8		

WO145/3145/7

204 Machine Gun Company.

66TH DIVISION
199TH INFY BDE

204TH MACHINE GUN COY.
MAR 1917 - FEB 1918

Vol 1

War Diary
of
204th Machine Gun Company
from
16th March to 31st March
1917.

Appendix.

A. T.P.R's
B. Operation Orders.
C. Casualty Returns.
D. Maps.

Volume 1.

To O.C. Major McCoop   29
    The following have been transferred from this unit
To No 7 Infection Hosp'l Malbassise ?1884 Pte Welby W.R. 21-3-17

                                            R. Stuart
                                            Capt James
21-3-17   for O.C. Both James Hith?
         I

O.C. 304 th Fld G.

The undermentioned has this day
been transferred to No. CCS

66376 Pte Mounsey J.W.

F W Hughes Capt
2nd i/c 2/2 E L Fd Amb

26.3.17

II

Army Form C. 2118.

Sheet 1

WAR DIARY
or
INTELLIGENCE SUMMARY.

(Erase heading not required.)

No. 224 Machine Gun Company

16th – 31st March 1917

Instructions regarding War Diaries and Intelligence Summaries are contained in F. S. Regs., Part II. and the Staff Manual respectively. Title pages will be prepared in manuscript.

Place	Date March	Hour	Summary of Events and Information	Remarks and references to Appendices
Le Havre	16th		The Company arrived at Le Havre about 10.0 a.m. from Southampton. The whole Company were unable to leave the harbour until about 1.0 p.m. We then marched onwards to No 2 Rest Camp.	Appx 1
No 2 Rest Camp Le Havre	17th	7.0 pm	Whole Company in Camp until results. One H.S. Wagon with one R.S.C. Driver and two heavy draught horses attached to the Company for baggage purposes.	Appx 2
Do	18th	9.30 a.m	Company entrained at Point 3, Gare des Marchandises for Bethune. Train left Station.	Appx 2
Bruay	19th	6.30 pm	Company arrived at Bethune and commenced detraining. Company's orders 190 Infantry Brigade to proceed to Bruay about 2½ miles from Bethune. Weather very wet.	Appx 3
D.H.	20th	2.0 a.m	Company took over 12 Mr. G. Emplacements in the support entrenchment of Cambrin Sector from the Loos Guns. The new Machine Gunners were Relieving the Line. Still snowing and stormy wind. Received orders from 199 Inf Brigade to move to Annequin.	Appx 4
Annequin	21st		Company Headquarters moved to Annequin.	Appx 5
"	22nd		One man evacuated out of Divisional Area, sick.	Appx 6
"	23rd		Very cold weather.	Appx 7
"	24th		Have first chance of showing the sights.	
"	25th		Very fine weather.	
		5.0 pm	Enemy shelled by bridge with 5.9 shells. No damage done. Received orders to relieve No 1 Gun Crew of the 110th Machine Gun Company in Vermelles Left Sector.	Appx 8

WAR DIARY or INTELLIGENCE SUMMARY

Army Form C. 2118.

No 201 Machine Gun Company
16th – 31st March 1917

Place	Date	Hour	Summary of Events and Information	Remarks and references to Appendices
Annequin	26th	7.30 pm	Indirect overhead fire employed by two of our guns when enemy communication trenches.	
do	26th	3.30 h	Relief of four guns of the 110th M.G. Coy carried out in Strongpoint sector. Shmary. One man wounded out of Devonraul Lines. Sick Pet. J. Houston. 17	
do	27th	5.30 pm	No 203 Machine Gun Company relieved 6 gun guns in the Cambrin left sector. Very wet. Strongpoint	
do	28th	2.30 pm	Four more gun placers in the Cambrin Sub in the village line. Two reinforcements arrived from the Base.	
do	29th		Three reinforcements (Armrs) arrived from Ashwill. Still very wet.	
do	30th	5.0 pm	Enemy again shelled by Hyppo. One shell burst off Bloomerie in corner of Stone House. 5.9 shell used again.	
do	31st		Company Headquarters moved to Noyelles. Enemy shelled the village a lot yesterday and today.	

Appendix "C"

Casualty Returns.

To. D.A.G
3rd Echelon G.H.Q

Attached please find
copy of war diary for the
month of April.

R B Buchanan
CAPTAIN
COMDG. No. 204 M.G. COY.

WAR DIARY

OF

204 MACHINE GUN COMPANY

FROM APRIL 1st TO APRIL 30th 1917

APPENDIX
(a) ~~T.P.R.~~
(b) OPERATION ORDERS
(c) ~~CASUALTY RETURNS~~
(d) ~~MAPS~~

Sheet 1.   April, 1917.

Army Form C. 2118.

WAR DIARY
or
INTELLIGENCE SUMMARY
(Erase heading not required.)

Instructions regarding War Diaries and Intelligence Summaries are contained in F.S. Regs., Part II. and the Staff Manual respectively. Title Pages will be prepared in manuscript.

No. 204 Machine Gun Company

Place	Date April	Hour	Summary of Events and Information	Remarks and references to Appendices
Noyelle	1st		Very wet in the afternoon evening. Everything quiet.	R.D. to
"	2nd		Very cold, windy with some snow.	R.D. to
"	3rd	3.0-3.15 a.m.	Brigade here a Gas attack Test. Enemy shelled the village a little during the day. Two our wounded in the morning but fine in the afternoon.	R.D. to
"	4th		One O.R. wounded by sniper in the leg. Three O.R's evacuated into Divisional Area. Attack off the strength of the company.	R.D. to
"	5th		However few employed on German communications. A beautiful day. An reinforcement arrived from hospital.	R.D. to
"	6th		Sniper few employed during the night on German communications. Two reinforcements arrived from Bairus. Slight shelling of Noyelle by the enemy — no damage done.	R.D. to
"	7th		Enemy began to shell Noyelle about the middle of the morning & am times for about an hour — no damage.	R.D. to
"	8th		Fine weather continues. Intermittent shelling of the village by the Boche. Still very fine.	R.D. to
"	9th		One N.C.O. sent to the Divisional Gas School at Bairus for 4 days. Showery with some hail. Enemy very quiet. The front north and south of Arras commenced and Vimy ridge taken.	R.D. to
"	10th		Very wet with some snow. Two O.Rs arrived from Bairus as reinforcements. Everything quiet.	R.D. to

Army Form C. 2118.

Sheet 2

WAR DIARY
or
INTELLIGENCE SUMMARY
(Erase heading not required.)

April 1917

No. 2 Bn. Machine Gun Company

Place	Date April	Hour	Summary of Events and Information	Remarks and references to Appendices
Noyelles	11th		Weather very changeable with a strong wind. One O.R. slightly wounded in the neck by shrapnel while acting as orderly. Still at church.	T.D. L.
"	12th		Very wet with much snow and sleet and a strong wind. Situation quiet.	R.D. L.
"	13th		Weather milder. Situation unchanged.	R.D. L.
"	14th		Very fine but windy. Considerable aeroplane activity. Situation quiet.	R.D. L.
"	15th		Stormy and wet. Enemy very quiet.	R.D. L.
"	16th		Stormy & very wet in the evening. Situation unchanged.	R.D. L.
"	17th		Fine and rain. Enemy motors enemy machine gun.	R.D. L.
"	18th		Weather unchanged.	
"	19th		One officer and one O.R. transferred. One officer and one officer from 10's M.G. Coy taken on strength to-day. Brent went to take our observer from 4 P.M. to 2nd August. During the night indirect fire employed on enemy communications. Weather changeable but milder.	R.D. L.
"	20th		Fine and hazy. During the day or night considerable machine gun employed on enemy Field Kitchen situated in the village of Quéry north of the Kitchen - Le Barais road.	R.D. L.
"	21st		Beautiful weather again. Our shoots, 6 to South y. charged with direction and short Lockel officer for and 3 O.Rs arrive in reinforcements from Carriers. We are now one officer and one O.R. over establishment.	R.D. L.
"	22nd			R.D. L.
"	23rd			R.D. L.

Sheet 3. April 1917. Army Form C. 2118.

WAR DIARY
or
INTELLIGENCE SUMMARY
(Erase heading not required.)

No. 204 Machine Gun Company

Place	Date April	Hour	Summary of Events and Information	Remarks and references to Appendices
Nœux les Mines	24th		Beautiful weather continues. Orders received from Brigade for Gas Attack N. and S. of the Bassée canal, to take place on the night of 25th/26th April, by the No. 4 (S) Coy R.E. and T(S) Coy R.E. On arrival report by the company for cooperation with above.	R.D. See appendix I
"	25th		Dull but fine. Gas attack, as above, postponed for 24 hours owing to the wind being unfavourable. Enemy normally quiet.	R.D. &c.
"	26th		Fine weather continues. Gas attack again postponed for 2 hours. Six I m guns opened up on the village of Hulluch & district in cooperation. For the first half hour very heavy fire was kept up. Afterwards hundred shots were fired until daylight.	R.D. &c
"	27th	2.10 am	Gun reported. Dull but fine. In the morning very warm in the afternoon. Received orders that tonight gas attack would be repeated, gone from 199th Brigade. The company orders for cooperation were also repeated, the guns to 10.0 pm. The company moved for cooperation and the attack were being commenced accordingly. The animal being favourable the attack was launched at 10.0 pm in front. The enemy apparently did not expect this repetition of the attack and showed no signs of alarm. Our guns opened intense fire in the same targets as the previous night. A gas attack was also launched by the 16th Brigade on our right. We did not cooperate. Four officers of the Heavy Branch, M.G.C., on a tour of instruction, joined the company to day. They are attached to us until further notice.	R.D. &c

Army Form C. 2118.

WAR DIARY
or
INTELLIGENCE SUMMARY.

(*Erase heading not required.*)

Sheet H. April 1917

No. 10th Machine Gun Company

Instructions regarding War Diaries and Intelligence Summaries are contained in F. S. Regs., Part II. and the Staff Manual respectively. Title pages will be prepared in manuscript.

Place	Date April	Hour	Summary of Events and Information	Remarks and references to Appendices
Nopelles	28th		Beautiful weather. Situation normal.	R.D. K.
	29th		Beautiful weather continues. Enemy sent over a large number of gas shells around Nieuville, some landing near Nopelles. This was probably in retaliation for our two gas attacks. Very warm and sunny. Enemy very quiet.	R.D. K.
"	30th		Branch M.G.C. have now two sections & platoons in the line.	R.D. K.

APPENDIX I   Sheet 1

204 Machine Gun Company

Special Orders   24-4-17

I. N°4(S) Coy R.E. and F(S) Coy R.E. will make an attack N. & S. of the LA BASSEE CANAL on the night of 25/26th April 1917. ZERO hour will be 12 midnight.

II. (a) "Gas alert" will be put on at 11.30 p.m. and will remain "ON" until ordered "OFF" by C.O's battalions.

(b) Should weather conditions not be favourable at 12.0 midnight all teams will "stand by" until operation is carried out or orders for its postponement are received through the Infantry. Where guns are isolated arrangements should be made for them to be warned.

(c) Special attention must be paid to soaking of anti-gas blankets etc. but too much reliance should not be placed in the blankets.

Sheet 2.

3. The following Machine Guns will open fire at ten minutes past ZERO and fire kept up for half an hour barrage fire.

Then occasional bursts until daylight. Officers concerned will warn O.C. of Battalion.

No 1 & 2 Sections { V45 Area around A.23.c.66.70
                  { V48 Cross roads at A.23.a.40.60
                        and midway junction approx
                  (R64(all) Enfilade from A.23.a.20.50
                        to A.23.c.60.70.

No 3 Section Central Keep Traverse AUCHY VILLAGE

No 4 Section { R.53 Target No 10.
             { R.54 ESTAMINET & neighbourhood
                        in A.29.a

4. Watches must be at Coy. H.Qrs not later than 8.45 p.m. to be synchronised.

5. The usual precautions must be taken & all calculations must be checked.

6. Acknowledge.

20th M.G. Coy H.Q.
24-4-17

To. H.Q. 34th Inf. Bde.

Attached please find copy of the War Diary of this Company for period May 1st – 31st / incl.

K.B. Buchanan
CAPTAIN
COMDG. No. 204 M.G. COY.

Confidential

WAR DIARY

OF

204 MACHINE GUN COMPANY

FROM

May 1st TO May 31st 1917.

~~APPENDICES.~~

+ ~~OPERATIONS~~

Sheet I   WAR DIARY or INTELLIGENCE SUMMARY   May 1917   Army Form C. 2118.

2nd Machine Gun Coy.

Place	Date	Hour	Summary of Events and Information	Remarks and references to Appendices
Noyelles	May 1st		Beautiful weather. The enemy's artillery retaliated the Reserve Trench in Bavrin Right Sub-Sector between 5-10 p.m. & 9.0 p.m. One of our guns were damaged. The gun was in its Indoor emplacement which was knocked in by an 8" shell. Laurie fire employed during night. The enemy's communication trenches were quiet.	R.D.
"	2nd 3rd		Very hot and fine. The day has been quiet. Hot weather continues. Considerable enemy activity on both sides. Quiet during the day but considerable enemy artillery activity during evening and night. Reviews made from Brigade H.Q. that the four officers of the Heavy Trench M.G.B. attached to this Company, were to proceed to the XIII Corps' Schools on St. Eloi in the M.G. War.	R.D.
"	4th 5th		Weather still very warm and fine. A quiet day. Very hot and sultry in the morning some rain and thunder in the afternoon. A quiet day. Enemy artillery retaliation.	R.D. R.D.
"	6th		Very fine with strong breezy showing. Noyelles shelves - quiet day. Paid O.R. under arrest awaiting trial by F.G.C.M., sent to Bois for observation as to mental condition.	R.D. R.D.
"	7th			R.D.
"	8th		Still quiet. Rain towards evening. Wind N. to N.W. during the night to about 10. M.P.H.	R.D.

2449 Wt. W14957/M90 750,000 1/16 J.B.C. & A. Forms/C.2118/12.

Army Form C. 2118.

Sheet No. 2.   WAR DIARY   May 1917

or

INTELLIGENCE SUMMARY

(Erase heading not required.)

Place	Date	Hour	Summary of Events and Information	Remarks and references to Appendices
Noyelles	May 9th		Beautiful weather again. 279 twice Frenchmen returned from Civil-Bivouacs. Bivouacs at Le Touquet. Very quiet day.	R.D.
"	10th		It turns out — evacuated out of Divisional Area. A quiet day. Enemy O.P.'s active. Fire directed. Enemy on intervals during the day on enemy communications.	R.D.
"	11th		Hot weather continues — a quiet day, except for enemy shelling on the ANNEQUIN – NOYELLES road by the enemy. Some incendiary shells were put over his huts in the open. Those active fire employed on enemy communications.	R.D.
"	12th		Very hot and very sultry and very quiet. Enemy fire employed by us on enemy communications during the day & night. Our aeroplane engaged by one of own guns. No machine was it manage.	R.D.
"	13th		Very hot and sultry with tendency to thunder. Heavy thunderstorm during the night. Heavy fire employed on enemy communications during the day.	R.D.
"	14th		Dull and not in afternoon. Very quiet. Lewis fire again employed on enemy communications. Two hostile aeroplanes engaged our division Off. Our returned and fired there bursts	R.D.

Sheet 3

Army Form C. 2118.

WAR DIARY
or
INTELLIGENCE SUMMARY
(Erase heading not required.)

204 Machine Gun Coy

May 1917

Instructions regarding War Diaries and Intelligence Summaries are contained in F.S. Regs., Part II. and the Staff Manual respectively. Title Pages will be prepared in manuscript.

Place	Date May	Hour	Summary of Events and Information	Remarks and references to Appendices
Noyelles	15th		Early this morning, 3.15 a.m. we carried out a M.G. demonstration against the Enemys movement areas. Seven guns took part. Very quiet all day. One O.R. received an re-inforcement.	28 2/Lts
	16th		Dull & wet. A very quiet day. 4 O.Rs struck off the strength during the week.	28 2/Lts
	17th		At 3.0 p.m. today our guns cooperated with Brigade Trench Mortars Stokes by firing indirectly on enemys communications. Enemy very quiet. Dull & wet.	28 2/Lts
	18th		Hostile aeroplanes flying at low altitudes over our lines were engaged by our guns and forced to retire. Some of them retaliated with M.G. fire but without effect. Dull with sunshine at intervals. A very quiet day.	28 2/M
	19th		Fine & warm. Fairly quiet day. Two O.R. wounded by shellfire one slightly, one rather seriously. Both successfully evacuated. Bright & hot. Lt. Darby proceeded to Cameron on leave. 9/M	28 2/Lts
	20th		Bright hot sun. Duties of Adjutant during his absence Captain Shaw referred to. Prior to his leaving for microscopic repairs Our A.A. guns fired at some them off. Fairly quiet day.	28 2/Lts

WAR DIARY
or
INTELLIGENCE SUMMARY

(Erase heading not required.)

Army Form C. 2118.

Sheet 4

204 M.G. Coy

Place	Date MAY	Hour	Summary of Events and Information.	Remarks and references to Appendices
NOYELLES	21st		Dull but fine. Order. Inspection of Transport by O.C. Divisional Train. 3 O.R's returned to the Base as inefficient. 3 O.R's transferred to C.C.S. and struck off strength of Coy.	2S. y/M
	22nd		Rained during morning. M.G's co-operated in daylight raid by means of indirect fire on enemy tracks in with it, is believed for good results. no Several heavy shells fell in neighbourhood of our emplacement during the afternoon. On O.R. reported for Corps Rest Station & 2 O.R. from re-inforcements Base.	2S. y/M
	23rd		Fine & warm. Considerable amount of hostile aeroplane activity during evening. Very quiet day.	2S. y/M
	24th		Fine & warm. Our guns fire at hostile aeroplane. Unusually large number of hostile aeroplanes seen. Very quiet day.	2S. y/M
	25th		Fine & warm. Hostile artillery v. T.M. strafe during afternoon. One O.R. killed & one wounded by shell.	2S. y/M
	26th		Fine & warm. Gun teams "Stood to" for one hour while infantry raid (one.) was in progress. Enemy still employing indirect fire at night.	2S. y/M

Sheet 5.   204 M.G. Coy   Army Form C. 2118.

WAR DIARY
INTELLIGENCE SUMMARY
(Erase heading not required.)

Place	Date	Hour	Summary of Events and Information	Remarks and references to Appendices
NOYELLES	27.5.17	-	Fine & Warm. Usual relief carried out. Our A.A. guns fired at hostile aeroplanes & forced them to rise sufficiently high to be engaged by our A.A. Batteries.	JS
	28.5.17		Fine & warm. Coy. Sgt. Major sent to Field Amb. by M.O. 2/5 Manchester Regt. Quiet day.	JS
	29.5.17		Dull & cool. Very quiet day. Coy. Sgt. Major transferred to No. 58 L.L.S. & struck off strength of Coy. accordingly. Nothing of importance.	JS
	30.5.17		Brighter in afternoon. Dull in morning.	JS
	31.5.17		Usual relief carried out. 3 O.R. reinforcements received from Base. Enemy still using indirect M.G. fire at night. Quiet day.	JS

4

Orderly Room — Date 3-7-17 — No. 204 M.G. Coy., M.G.C.

To OC 3rd Echelon

attached please find
copy of "WAR DIARY" for
the 204th Machine Gun Coy
for month ending June 30th
1917

R B Buchanan
———————————— CAPTAIN
COMDG. No. 204 M G COY.

WAR DIARY

OF

204 MACHINE GUN COMP.Y

FROM 1st June 1917 TO 30 June 1917.

APPENDIX

a. RELIEF ORDERS

Sheet I

Army Form C. 2118.

WAR DIARY
or
INTELLIGENCE SUMMARY
(Erase heading not required.)

June 1917

No. 204 Machine Gun Company

Place	Date June	Hour	Summary of Events and Information	Remarks and references to Appendices
NOYELLES	1st		Fine and hot. A few shells in neighbourhood of Noyelles in the morning. No damage done. 2 O.R.'s wounded in trench.	R.O.Lr
"	2nd		A quiet day.	R.O.Lr
"	3rd		Very fine and warm. Enemy very quiet, but nights our guns kept him from gaps in enemy's wire made by artillery during the day. Beautiful weather. Sgt. Lunn accidentally shot Pte. Hutchinson this morning whilst cleaning his revolver. Pte. Hutchinson badly wounded. Sgt. Lunn remanded for Court Martial and Summary of Evidence taken.	R.O.Lr
"	4th		R.G.C. Portion, Bamforton Sgt. Sexton, Phelan Corp. afternoon. Hope Simm sent to A.D.S. suffering from bad shell shock. 2 O.R.'s reported from Base a reinforcements Very hot. Corpl. Kennett provided with England to join a Cadet School. T.66 position again shelled. Iron + Iron movement to an alternative position. One slight case of shell shock.	R.O.Lr
"	5th			
"	6th		Very hot. Enemy quiet.	R.O.Lr
"	7th		One reinforcement, a Transport driver, reported to-day.	R.O.Lr
"	8th		Very cloudy and dull, with some showers. First A. Daily returned from M.S. School away at Camiers. 15 of 3rd Manchester made unsuccessful attack on enemy line. We assisted with barrage fire. Account arrived. Annals again complete.	R.O.Lr

Army Form C. 2118.

Sheet 2. June 1917

WAR DIARY
or
INTELLIGENCE SUMMARY.
(Erase heading not required.)

No. 204th Machine Gun Company

Place	Date	Hour	Summary of Events and Information	Remarks and references to Appendices
NOYELLES	9/6		During enemy retaliation for last nights raid, two O.R's were wounded. This morning L/Cpl Newell G and Sgt Shelley were wounded by a rifle grenade. A very fine day. Enemy very quiet.	R.D.L.
"	10/6		Dull but cool. Enemy quiet. This evening an aeroplane with bombs had fire with trigger cord on one light. One O.P. returned from base last station. One O.R. proceeded on leave.	
"	11/6		Very wet. Enemy quiet. An aeroplane engaged and driven off. Advance fire employed in enemy communications. Received orders that 12th M.G. Squadron at Cavalry Barracks would take over 12 emplacements. Relief orders issued.	R.D.L. See appendix 1
"	12/6		Very hot and thundery. 12th M.G. Squadron relieved 12 of 1st squad of the company. A Company in rest at NOYELLES for a week or ten days, with the exception of two teams. One gun opened fire on hostile aeroplane causing it to return over its own lines. Enemy quiet.	R.D.L.
"	13/6		Fine shot. One gun engaged on enemy aeroplane causing it to turn and disappear over its own lines.	
"	14/6		Beautiful weather. A quiet period. One gun engaged a hostile aeroplane causing it to return over its own lines.	R.D.L.

Sheet 3

WAR DIARY June 1917

INTELLIGENCE SUMMARY

Army Form C. 2118.

No. 204th Machine Gun Coy

Place	Date	Hour	Summary of Events and Information	Remarks and references to Appendices
NOYELLES	June 15th		Very hot and sultry. Company training continued. Indirect fire on enemy's communications carried out last night. Our O.R. sent on leave. Two officers, 2/Lt Albrecht + 2/Lt Rushington reported from Base Depôt.	T.D. to
"	16th		Very quiet.	R.D. to
"	17th		Very hot and sultry. Enemy very quiet. We fired 10000 rounds on enemy's movement areas.	R.D. to
"	18th		Very hot and sultry. In the afternoon a very heavy thunder storm preceded by a dust storm — a quiet period. The two watch duty men sent to the 2/3rd East Lancs F.A. for course on Water Duties. Two R.A.M.C men attached to replace. Received preliminary orders re relief of Brigade at end of month. Nominal strength of the company is now 166.	R.D. to
"	19th		Rain at intervals. Enemy very quiet. Our O.R. struck off the strength.	R.D.As.
"	20th		Still wet. Enemy quiet. Received orders re the relief of this company by the 99th M.S. Coy on the 21.6.17. This company to proceed to Marles by Mines. 8. O.R.s reported as reinforcements from Base Depôt.	R.D. to
MARLES LEZ MINES	21st		Relief completed. Company left NOYELLES about 5.0 p.m and marched to MARLES LEZ MINES, arriving about 9.30 p.m.	R.D. to
"	22nd		Billeting arrangements made, latrines etc, dug. Stores overhauled. Received orders to move on Monday 25th to H XV Corps Area at DUNKIRK. 2/Lt Albrecht + 2/Lt Rushington posted to 146th M.S. Coy.	R.D. to
"	23rd		H.J.C. transferred by H XI Corps to H 146th M.S. Coy. Limber packed. 2/Lt Albrecht + 16. preparations for move on Monday at 3.0 a.m. transferred from the 146th Machine Gun Company.	R.D. to

WAR DIARY

Sheet 4

June 1917

INTELLIGENCE SUMMARY

(Erase heading not required.)

Army Form C. 2118.

No. 20th Machine Gun Coy.

Place	Date	Hour	Summary of Events and Information	Remarks and references to Appendices
MARLES LES MINES	24th		Preparation for move tomorrow morning pending.	R.D. hr
ST. POL SUR MER	25th		Company entrained at Chocques at 4.30 a.m. Train moved off at 7.33 a.m. and arrived at LOON PLAGE at 10.30 a.m. Detained marched to St. Pol-sur-Mer.	R.D. hr
"	26th		Billeting arrangements made. Programme of work drawn up.	R.D. hr
"	27th		Company training. Some kind chill landed in DUNKERQUE and MALO-LES-BAINS. 7k guns went to St. Pol. refield. One O.R. returned from leave. One O.R. reinforcement reported from Base Depot.	R.D. hr
"	28th		Company training. Thursday all day and very wet in afternoon and evening. 2nd Lieut Swart W. strength from the 2.6.17. 2nd Lt Pinchington H., 2 Lt Smart from the 15.6.17. supernumerary officer, taken on the strength via 2/Lt Swart Base Depot. On.	R.D. hr
"	29th		Drill was not at intervals. Company training continued. 2 M.G.O.s reported from Base Depot. On.	R.D. hr
"	30th		Very wet. Training continued. O.R. returned from Course of Instruction at Camiers. Nominal strength of the Company is now 10 Officers and 170 O.Rs.	R.D. hr

SECRET   Copy No 8

Special Relief Orders by Captain R.B. Buchanan Commanding 204 Machine Gun Company

1. The 1st M.G. Squadron, 1st Cavalry Division will relieve 7 g.m. of the 204th M.G. Company in the CAMBRIN SECTORS on the 10th inst.

2. The Sub-section of No 1 Section at V.4.8 and V.4.5 positions will not be relieved until further orders.

3. Guides, one man from each gun team, will be at their respective Section HdQrs at 5.0 p.m. (Guide from RAILWAY EMPLACEMENT report at H.Q. HARTS ALLEY.)

4. Receipt will be obtained for all trench stores, aeroplane sights, aeroplane photos, maps, charts etc., one copy of such receipts being handed over to the incoming officer the other sent to company H.Q. The positions of Boche "tender spots" such as bricks, tramways, popular Communication Trenches, transport routes should be pointed out.

5. 10 Belt Boxes per gun will be handed over to the incoming gun teams.

6. All emplacements and dugouts must be handed over in a perfectly clean and sanitary condition.

7. Strict instructions must be given to gun commanders that they must be thoroughly satisfied that the gun commander taking over understands exactly the line of fire, S.O.S., positions of neighbouring guns, or anything peculiar to the emplacement or ground in front.

8. O.C. No 1 Section will particularly point out the danger of movement or fire at the RLY EMPLACEMENT

9. One officer per section of the 204th Company will remain at each of the Section H.Q. during the night of 12th-13th inst. One O.R. per section will also remain behind during the night of the 12th-13th to guide ration parties to the distributing point. They will return to NOYELLES on the morning of the 13th inst.

10. On completion of the relief all ranks will return to NOYELLES.

11. Completion of relief will be reported by sections to Company Headquarters as soon as possible.

12. Acknowledge.

Joseph Darby
Lieut & Adjutant
204 Machine Gun Coy

Distribution
Copy No 1. H.Q. 199th Infantry Bgde.
" 2. O.C. 1st M.G. Squadron, 1st Cavalry Divn
" 3. O.C. No.1 Section
" 4. O.C. No.2 "
" 5. O.C. No.3 "
" 6. O.C. No.4 "
" 7. War Diary
" 8. "
" 9. "
" 10. File

To. H.Q.
   199th Infy Bgde

[ORDERLY ROOM stamp — Date 1.8.17 — No. 204 M.G. COY. M.G.C.]

Attached please find copy of "War Diary" for month ending July 31st 1917

R.B.Buchanan
CAPTAIN
COMDG. No. 204 M.G. COY.

CONFIDENTIAL

WAR DIARY

— OF —

204 MACHINE GUN COMPANY

From 1st July 1917. To 31st July 1917.

APPENDICES

I. Programme of Work
II. } Operation Orders.
III.}

Army Form C. 2118.

Sheet 1

WAR DIARY
or
INTELLIGENCE SUMMARY
(Erase heading not required.)

20th Machine Gun Company

July 1917

Place	Date	Hour	Summary of Events and Information	Remarks and references to Appendices
ST. POL SUR MER	1st July		Sunday – usual Church Parade. Fine and breezy.	R.D.L.
	2nd		Tactical Scheme in the morning – bathing in the afternoon. Dull but fine. Some Taubes twice flew over DUNKERQUE and ST. POL to-day, dropping bombs on the former town.	R.D.L.
	3rd		Firing stoppages on the sands. In the afternoon bathing. A beautiful day.	R.D.L.
	4th		Action from limbers and overhead drill. Dull + showery.	R.D.L.
	5th		Firing on sands with gun + rifles in morning. Bathing in the afternoon. Dull but fine	R.D.L.
	6th		Company training as per Programme of Work. L.S.M. McLean reported for duty on transfer from the 67th M.G. Coy. Our N.C.O. returned from 2nd Corps Infantry School. A beautiful day.	R.D.L.
	7th		Received orders to move on the 9/7/17 to new billeting area near TETEGHEM.	R.D.L.
	8th		Sunday – usual Church Parade. Very wet. 2/Lt Staff proceeded to TETEGHEM to procure billets for company.	R.D.L. R.D.L.
	9th		Company moved to TETEGHEM and billeted in a farm near the village.	R.D.L.
	10th		Company Training continued. Very fine weather.	
	11	12.30 a.m	Received orders at 12.30 a.m. that half the Coy was to prepare to move at 1 hour's notice. Stood by all day.	R.D.L.
		11.30	Received orders at 11.30 a.m. to proceed to GHYVELDE. Two reinforcements (O.R.s) arrived.	
			One O.R. admitted to hospital.	
GHYVELDE	12th		Half the Coy. proceeded to GHYVELDE under Lieut. DARBY and the other half proceeded to join the 216th M.G. Coy. under the command of the C.O.	R.D.L.
	13th		Company Training continued. One O.R. struck off strength, sick. One O.R. struck off strength – attached to 254th Div. Emp. Coy.	1

Army Form C. 2118.

WAR DIARY
or
INTELLIGENCE SUMMARY
(Erase heading not required.)

Sheet 1   July, 1917.

20th Machine Gun Company

Place	Date	Hour	Summary of Events and Information	Remarks and references to Appendices
GHYVELDE COXYDE BAINS	July 14th		Received orders to move to the COXYDE BAINS.	R.D.4.
	15th		The half company moved to COXYDE BAINS and reported to the other half company. The Defence of the 16 mat from ST IDESBALDE - NIEUPORT BAINS taken over from the 3rd M.G. Coy. Fourteen guns placed in the line.	R.D.4.
Do.	16th		Arrangements for defence of line inspected and necessary repairs noted.	R.D.4. R.D.4.
Do.	17th		New work commenced. Several emplacements begun. Weather fine.	R.D.4.
Do.	18th		Very quiet. Work in line continued. Very wet.	R.D.4.
Do.	19th		Dull. Sun fine. Very quiet.	R.D.4.
Do.	20th		Received orders in relief of company by the 96th M.G. Coy and instructions re duties to be taken out. Eight Guns of the company, the employed on Labour workers and convoy Guns I from positions behind the line. Positions reconnoitred. Relief of the coy completed during the night.	R.D.4.
Do.	21st		One N.C.O. reinforcement arrived and an attached to the company for instruction. Nos 1 & 2 Sections moved up the line to take up positions chosen yesterday. Weather still very fine.	R.D.4.
Do.	22nd		A beautiful day. Considerable shelling round our guns in morning and evening. One artillery action also. We return a small workers fire on enemy's own municipals. One O.R. wounded. Considerable shelling round our guns in the morning. Our artillery very active.	R.D.4.
Do.	23rd		Enemy fairly quiet during the morning. Heavy artillery fire by last side in afternoon and evening. Heavy navel gun ammo at night.	R.D.4.
Do.	24th		During the night at 1.30 a.m a gas attack was launched. We cooperated with heavy machine gun fire. A second discharge was thrown out at 2.30 a.m., a similar support by our guns. We fired altogether 60000 rounds with eight guns. (See appendix II for Operation Orders). We find during day.	R.D.4. Appx. See Appendix II

2449 W. W14957/M90 750,000 (1/16 H.B.C. & A. Forms/C.2118/12.

Sheet III

WAR DIARY
or
INTELLIGENCE SUMMARY

Army Form C. 2118.

July 1917

234 Machine Gun Company

Place	Date	Hour	Summary of Events and Information	Remarks and references to Appendices
COXYDE BAINS	July 25th		A quiet day. Nos 1 & 2 Sections were relieved by No 3 & 4 Sections in the afternoon. Moved harassing fire employed during the night. Enemy reasonably quiet. A fair amount of counter battery work by both sides.	R.D. &c.
Do.	26th		One machine gun hung during at the Watering Troughs got ..... pretty hot at times. Overhead indirect fire again employed during the night. About 1.0 a.m. our guns opened fire on the S.O.S sent by the Right Sector (i.e. the sector down to the sea). 11,000 rounds were fired. Beautiful weather continues.	R.D. &c.
Do.	27th		Received orders for operation "Xa" (see appendix III) and further orders were prepared for zero minus before zero a message was received cancelling the operations.	R.D. &c. [III]
Do.	28th		Very hot and fine. Our guns positions becoming too hot owing to enemy's counter battery work, and positions were reconnoitred and two new laid out. Eight shelter emplacements were dug. The targets hung fired on a Taleyran barrage of some the gun attack .... last night was hopeless for that night. We carried out nearly the whole of our programme before receiving the message from the artillery cancelling the operations. From 12.0 Midnight to 4.0 a.m. a considerable amount of gas shell (some of the new mustard type) fell in the neighbourhood of our positions. By respirators had to be worn during the firing. Our O.R. evacuated apparently suffering from gas. Twenty hundred rounds was with a long range machine gun a day.	R.D. &c. The operation orders are appendix ...

Army Form C. 2118.

Sheet IV

WAR DIARY

July 1917

INTELLIGENCE SUMMARY.

(Erase heading not required.)

20th Machine Gun Company

Place	Date	Hour	Summary of Events and Information	Remarks and references to Appendices
Coudekerque (Coxyde) Bains	July 29th		Weather — very fine. The guns with which the enemy bombards Coxyde Bains is a 5.9" high velocity gun, probably naval. A considerable number of shells were fired at intervals of about three hours all day. One O.R. killed by one of them. Counter-battery went to the enemy works on Lombartzyde Peninsula, but not as bad as the former situation. Heavy shelling in evening advanced H.Qrs. 30 O.Rs. evacuated. Naval programme of bombarding the enemy carried out during the night. Some casualty shelling on the main Oost Dunkerke — Nieuport road.	R.D. br
Do.	30.		Bains went on artillery advanced bombardment Coxyde = Bains. This has been about 40000. Enemy very quiet during the day. Fine weather. Enemy used the night on enemy "Twelve Spots". These + other "places of habit" were fired during the night.	R.D. br
Do.	31st		A beautiful day. Slight shelling around on gun position which was quickly silenced. Some of our artillery fire. The strength at the beginning of the month was 10 Officers and 168 O.Rs. any at the end of the month is 10 Officers and 168 O.Rs. Four O.R. reinforcements were received during the month.	R.D. br

Appendix I Programme of Work Week Ending 7th July

	9-0 – 10-0	10-0 – 11-0	11-0 – 12-0	12 – 1-30
Monday	Ceremonial Drill	Action from Limbers & pack saddle		
Tuesday	S.A.A.	S.A.A.	Indirect Fire	Stripping & Repairs
Wednesday	Lecture	Tactical Schemes		
Thursday	Musketry & Regular Practice	Squad Drill	Rough Ground Care & Drill Cleaning	
Friday	Tests of Elementary Training Section	Pack Saddle Drill	Musketry & Revolver Practice	Iron Helmet Drill
Saturday	Section Schemes	Tactical Scheme	Cleaning S.A.A. Machine Guns Ammunition & Belts	Ann. ammgths & Stores

Joseph Darby
Lieut & Adjutant,
No. 204 Machine Gun Co.

Appendix I   Programme of Work

Week Ending 14 July 1917.

	9.0 – 10.0	10.0 – 11.0	11.0 – 12.0	12.0 – 1.30
Monday	S.A.	Barrage Fire & Turning Guns		
Tuesday	Selecting & Judging Gun Drill	Tactical Schemes with Sections		
Wednesday	Antitank Drill	Shell Hole Emplacements		
Thursday	I.O.E.T.	S.A.	Indirect Fire Searching Fire	
Friday	Half Company Tactical Scheme			
Saturday	Belt Filling Machine	Overhauling & cleaning S.A.A. & Stores		

Gas Drill each morning 6.0 – 6.30
Lectures (NCOs – Fire Direction Map Reading Vickers Daily
    Men – General

                                    Lieut & Adjutant
                                    No. 204 Machine Gun Co

"Appendix II"

Machine Gun Fire Table

PHASE	SECTION	TARGETS	TIMES OF FIRING	ROUNDS PER GUN PER MINUTE	ROUNDS REQUIRED PER GUN	ROUNDS PER SECTION
1	RIGHT (No 1)	M14b 6.3 M14b 6.1 M15a 05.30 M15d 25.45 M15d 0.5 M15d 1.7	9.30 to ZERO − 30 mins ZERO − 30 mins to ZERO − 25 mins ZERO − 25 mins to ZERO − 20 mins	20 30 40	6,650	27,400
1	LEFT (No 2)	M14b 9.5 6.0 M15a 25.6.0 M15a 5.3 M15a 4.4 M15a 8.8 M15d 9.5	ZERO − 20 mins to ZERO − 5 mins ZERO − 5 mins to ZERO − 2 mins ZERO − 2 mins to ZERO + 3 mins	50 100 250		
2	RIGHT AND LEFT	BARRAGE LINE from M9c 0.0 to M6c 0.0	ZERO + 61 mins to ZERO + 67 mins	250	1500	6,000
3	RIGHT AND LEFT	as in PHASE 1	ZERO + 80 mins to 3.0 am	40	400	1,600
					8,750	35,000
						70,000

Appendix III   Machine Gun Fire Table

SECTION	TARGET No	AREA INCLUDED BY TARGET	TIME OF FIRING	No. OF ROUNDS PER GUN PER MINUTE	TOTAL No. OF ROUNDS PER GUN	TOTAL No. ROUNDS PER SECTION
3	1 (BLACK OUTLINE)	M14b 50.75. M14b 92.53. M14b 35.45. M14b 75.25	Z+2 to Z+5	250	750	
3	2 (BLACK OUTLINE)	M.8 d 85.10. M15a 20.90. M.14b 50.75. M14b 92.53	Z+6 to Z+10	100	400	14,600
3	3 (BLACK OUTLINE)	M.8 d 65.10. M15a 20.90. M14b 35.45. M14b 75	Z+50 to Z+65 / Z+70 to Z+75 / Z+100 to Z+105	100	2500	
4	1 (RED OUTLINE)	M 9c 10.10. M15a 75.75. M14b 60.65. M15a 50.35	Z+2 to Z+5	250	750	
4	2 (")	M 9c 25.45. M 9c 98.10. M 9c 10.10. M15a 75.75	Z+6 to Z+10	100	400	14,600
4	3 (")	M14b 80.65. M15a 60.35. M14b 30.70. M15a 30.0	Z+50 to Z+65 / Z+70 to Z+75 / Z+100 to Z+105	100	2500	

29,200

Vol 6

CONFIDENTIAL

WAR DIARY

— OF —

204 MACHINE GUN COY.

From 1st August 1917 to 31st August 1917.

VOL. VI

APPENDICES

III. Programme of Work.
II. } Tactical
IV. } Operation Orders.

Sheet 1

WAR DIARY
or
INTELLIGENCE SUMMARY
(Erase heading not required.)

Army Form C. 2118.

August 1917

No. 204 Machine Gun Company

Place	Date	Hour	Summary of Events and Information	Remarks and references to Appendices
(OXY)EPAINE	1st		Company in training for attack. Preparation of emplacements for offensive progressing. Very little enemy artillery fire. One battery exposed all day. Very wet.	R.D.L.
Do.	2nd		Very wet and visibility poor. S.A.A. stores were dumped in preparation for offensive. Details of target drawn & prepared. Enemy's western front the average trenches in a offensive on moving forward. Much artillery fire.	R.D.L.
Do.	3rd		Very wet in the next to four. Our trenches are nearly all under water. Enemy very quiet. One O.P. put in trench. No. 3rd Section relieved No. 1 & 2 Section in emergency for the last night complete. 11.30 a.m. Evacuation of Sub H.Q. Company attacked to no. for orgn. Infantry. Infantry advancing in accordance with programme of firing during the Barrage. Guns observed nothing of new Mortar Type. Left men in gun positions during the night.	R.D.L.
Do.	4th		Our artillery heavily active. Enemy artillery kept quiet. One O.P. moved up from lower occupied own trenches. Our men having trouble owing to mud any time.	R.D.L.
Do.	5th			R.D.L.
Do.	6th		Further activity in but otherwise normal.	R.D.L.
Do.	7th		One gun shell fell over ammo. dump. One 2 a.m. returned to the scene of action and moved to gift on about of the ong Barrage at 1.30 a.m. No main much placed home.	R.D.L.

WAR DIARY
INTELLIGENCE SUMMARY

Army Form C. 2118.

Sheet II August 1917

28th Machine Gun Company

Place	Date	Hour	Summary of Events and Information	Remarks and references to Appendices
(Coxy)2 BAINS	7th		Are operating with M.G. for S. Shutes Battn now Infantry S.S.	S.D.S.
Do.	8th		Enemy sent over a few gas shells in retaliation. Early in the morning this in the afternoon and evening. Enemy normal. Quiet. Relief made in afternoon. Engineer with a Projector Gas attack at 11.30 p.m. Order was issued for gas attack was cancelled. Route for	S.D.S.
Do.	9th		No 1,2 Section relieved No 3rd Section. Remaining on duty. Enemy Quiet. Reserve men in company when off duty went about in caravan II. Relief continues tonight. The company relieved 203 M.S. Coy in the station by 202 M.S. Coy. Habit enemy aeroplane very field over our	S.D.S.
Do.	10th		front line. 8.30 a.m. Station normal in handing the station to 202 M.S. Coy. in trenches. Enemy aeroplane over field over our lines during the day.	S.D.S.
Do.	11th		Station normal. Enemy very quiet. Shots sweeps. Enemy shelled COXYDE BAINS with a 5.0" H.V. gun from 12.0 M.N. night to 3.30 a.m. about 25 shells were sent on positions on the Shore killed. Some few shells fell near our position in the station. 3.0 a.m. the enemy starting on any quiet round the artillery activity in both sides. Heavy shelling fell between 10 & 5 p.m. especially near Rly Station NIEUPORT BAINS, the trench being blown in	R.D.S.
Do.	12th			R.D.S.

WAR DIARY / INTELLIGENCE SUMMARY

Army Form C. 2118.

August 1917

20th Machine Gun Company

Place	Date	Hour	Summary of Events and Information	Remarks and references to Appendices
(Oxy) Bains	13th		Weather fine. Unusual enemy artillery activity — tunnels knocked in at several places.	A.A.R.
Do.	14th		Gas shell fell near Coxyde positions from 1 A.M. – 3 A.M. Enemy aeroplane attempted to drop bombs on our batteries 5.10 – 5.45 A.M. Turn very heavy at 3 A.M. on Machine Gun tunnel & plank roads. Enemy unusually quiet. Weather stormy.	R.D.
Do.	15th		Usual enemy avial activity in early morning. Several planes engaged at intervals from 4.30 A.M. – 6.30 A.M. Enemy quiet all the day. The enemy artillery active on Nieuport Bains during afternoon.	
Do.	16th		Considerable enemy avial activity. 5 to 9 A.M. First aeroplane in morning. In the afternoon a number of planes over our front line. Relieved by 1st Sherwood Foresters.	R.D. A.A.R.
Do.	17th		Nieuport Bains gas shelled 12.30 A.M. – 1.30 A.M. 5.0 A.M. – 6.0 A.M. Enemy aeroplanes again engaged with A.A. guns. Enemy artillery active. Coxyde Bains shelled during the night. Batteries unmolested.	
Do.	18th		Considerable enemy avial activity. Many aeroplanes reported by our guns. Enemy artillery active on Nieuport – Nieuport Bains. Weather fine.	A.A.R.

Army Form C. 2118.

Sheet IV

August 19 1

WAR DIARY
or
INTELLIGENCE SUMMARY
(Erase heading not required.)

No. 246 Mahine Gun Company

Place	Date	Hour	Summary of Events and Information	Remarks and references to Appendices
CORDE BOIS	19th		Several aeroplanes engaged during early part of the day. In afternoon all our aeroplanes forced back or shaved off by a Hun Camp Plane artillery aircraft fuerat.	
Do.	20th		From every aeroplane one shot guns to bear — firing every moment. Six Jun Cons of the company relieved by 243 Coy for 24 hours at 5 a.m. Relief completed 11.30 a.m. in spite of Company keeping during the evening. Weather still very fine. Some very severe actions in the evening.	
Do.	21st		Several planes down from Lenham & stopped by Company about 18 Sep by our guns of 202 M.G.Cy, along the sunny Valley Roubert 8.15 p.m. Company continued employed as per programme of work — one Section Officers III Libs five Kin	
Do.	22nd		Some much movement of dunkown nature among the men and Horses of the Company was observed. Several other ranks admitted to aid Station. Dug out hits at COPSE BOIS and	
Do.	23rd		Shells of the kind as explanation against the men's shelling they are not now the best of my knowledge	
Do.	24th		Discovery — having received no word of possible.	
Do.	25th		foreign reliance of known tanks to brew as I myself	
Do.	26th		No information of the R.E's until further orders	
Do.	27th		They are a Company coming actually by writing trains	

WAR DIARY
or
INTELLIGENCE SUMMARY

(Erase heading not required.)

Army Form C. 2118.

Sheet V   August 1917   No. 368 Heavy Battery Group Southern

Place	Date	Hour	Summary of Events and Information	Remarks and references to Appendices
OXYDE BAINS	29th Aug		Heavy wet event returning. Enemy shelled COXYDE BAINS during the evening for about an hour from 9.0 p.m. — 10.0 p.m.	Ref.
Do.	30th		Still very wet and stormy. Infantry training on trench work on firing ranges. Reconnaissances taken over. Honors duties in the 19.17.	
Do.	31st		Still wet. Six Officers attended a Lecture on Barrages made by the XV Corps School by Major Berry M.C. of O.M.S. South Down School C/M 15 RS. The average strength of the company on the 1st August were 10 Officers and 168 other ranks and on the 31st August were 10 Officers and 179 other ranks.	Rpt.

Appendix II

SECRET

Relief Orders by Capt. R.B. Buchanan   Copy No.
Commanding No. 204 M.G. Coy.
NIEUPORT 1:10,000   9.5.17

1. The 204th M.G. Coy. will relieve the 203rd M.G. Coy. in the NIEUPORT BAINS Sector on the 10th inst. Relief to be completed by 9.0. a.m.

2. The 203rd M.G. Coy will relieve the 204th M.G. Coy in the harassing fire positions.

3. The total number of guns for the line will be 13 made up as follows:-
   No 1 Section   3 Guns and Teams
   No 2   "   3   "   "
   No 3   "   3   "   "
   No 4   "   4   "   "

4. Guides for No.1 Section will be at the end of NEW AVENUE M.21.c.50.65 at 5.30 a.m.
   Guides for No.2 Section will be at the same place at 6.30 a.m.
   Guides for No. 3 & 4 Sections will be at H.Q. 203 M.G. Coy at 5.30 a.m.

5. Gun positions to be taken over are:-
   No.1 Section   R.11. R.12. R.13. (2 A.A. positions included)
   No.2   "   R.8. R.9. R.10. (at present held by 248 Coy attached 203)
   No.3   "   R.5. R.6. R.7
   No.4   "   R.1. R.2. R.3. R.4. (1 A.A. position included)

6. The necessary requirements for each gun will be 10 belt boxes, Spare Parts Box and wooden gun case.

7. All Secret Maps, Standing Orders etc., Ration Dumps Water Supplies will be taken over and a signature given and obtained. These French Store Lists are to be sent to Coy. H.Q. as soon as possible.

8. Advanced Coy. H.Q. will be in BATH AVENUE

9. Completion of relief will be reported to Advanced Coy. Hqrs. by 9.30 a.m. - not later.

10. As soon as possible Section Officers will report to the C.O.s of their respective Battalions.

11. Regarding para 2:- 2/Lt. Maunder will remain behind with one team each of Nos 1 & 2 Sections and finally hand over to 203 M.G. Coy. all targets Boxes S.A.A. Trench and "T" mountings, aeroplane mountings (not sights) will be handed over with any other information which would be useful.

12. Two limbered wagons will report to 2/Lt. R.P. Maunder at 10.0 a.m. when the two remaining gun teams will return to Coy. Hqrs. COXYDE-LES-BAINS. Great care must be taken that all property of this Company is returned in these limbers. Should the relieving sections of 203 Coy. not arrive by 10.0. a.m. 2nd Lieut Maunder will remain behind until such time as they do arrive.

13. Orders relating to BARRAGE FIRE will not be handed over, but the gun positions etc. will.

14. The half section of No 248 M.G. Coy. will return to CANADA BANKS arriving not later than 7.0. a.m.

Copies 1 OC No 1 Sect
2 " 2 "
3 " 32 "
4 " 3 "
5 " 4 "
6 T.O
7 File
8 } War Diary
9 }

(Sgd) R.B. Buchanan Capt
Commanding 204 M.G. Coy.

Correction above Relief Orders 9.8.17 paras. 2, 11 & 12
for 203 Coy read 202 Coy.

An officer of 202 Coy will report to you at 9.0. am. 10.8.17.

Appendix II

Programme of Work

24.6.17   16.30 9.17 (medium)

Day	5.30	7.0 – 7.30	8.45 – 10.0	10.0 – 11.0	11.15 – 12.0	12.0 – 12.30	Afternoon
Friday	Reveille	Gas drill	Barrage drill (Elementary)	Barrage drill (Elementary)	A.A. Lights	Care & cleaning of guns & S.A.A.	Bathing etc.
Saturday	"	"	Barrage drill	Arms drill	"	Care & cleaning of guns & S.A.A.	"
Sunday	"	"	Church Parades				"
Monday	"	"	Revolver Practice Bombing & A.A. Lights	I.A. (firing)	I.A. (firing)	"	"
Tuesday	"	"	Squad drill & saluting	Barrage drill	P.T.	"	"
Wednesday	"	"	I.A. and Mechanism	A.A. Lights	March with guns, tripods, S.A.A. etc.	"	"
Thursday	"	"	Arms drill & saluting	Barrage drill	P.T.	"	"

Appendix IV

Copy No. 4

Relief Orders.

1. The 201st M.G. Coy will be relieved by the 200th M.G. Coy in the NIEUPORT BAINS SECTOR on the nights of the 20th and 21st inst.

2. On the night of the 20th inst. 6 guns R1. 2. 3. 4. 5 & 6 under 2nd Lt. F.W. Scrapp will be relieved

3. One Guide from each Gun team will be at Section Hd Qrs at 9.45 pm.

4. On being relieved the teams will return to billets in COXYDE BAINS

5. 2 · P.S Limbered wagons will await these teams at M21c 30.70 about 100 yds from the "T" roads, from 11.15 pm.

6. All surplus stores may be dumped near this point earlier in the evening (stand to' must not be effected.) Guns, tripods, 6 belt boxes per gun, First aid cases and 1 spare part box must remain.

7. On the night of the 21st inst 2 gun teams under 2nd Lt.

5th 6/

R.P. Mander and the 4-Coast
Defence guns will be
relieved

8. 1- Guide per gun team from
the 2 guns of No 1 Section
will be at Adv Coy H.Q at
6.0 pm
1- Guide per gun team from
the Coast Defence guns will
be at LAITERIE ROYAL at 6.30
pm

9. para 6 applies to this relief
also
The whole of the H.Q. equipment
will be at the LAITERIE ROYALE
by 6.30 pm

10. On relief the gun teams & H.Q
will return to COXYDE BAINS

11. 3- S.S. limbers will be at
LAITERIE ROYAL arriving at
6.50 pm (for H.Q and surplus
store of No1 Section) 8.0 pm
and 8.20 pm respectively.

12. All Defence Schemes, Secret
Maps, Aeroplane Photographs
and Trench Stores of other
nature will be handed
over and receipts obtained
A copy of this list will be

sent to Adv. Coy H.Q. on
receipt of these orders

13. All reliefs will be reported
to Adv. Coy. H.Q. by runner.
A special runner will be
sent from Adv. Coy H.Q. to Section
H.Q. for the relief on the 20th
inst.

14. All dugouts and emplacements
must be left perfectly
clean. Latrines where possible
must be left empty.

15. Acknowledge.

Adv. Coy H.Q.
304 M.G. Coy.
20.8.17.

R B Buchanan
Capt
Cmdg. 304 M.G. Coy.

Copies
1. OC No 2 Sec.
2. OC No 1 . (acting)
3. OC No 3 .
4. Adjutant & S.O. c/o
5. T.O.
6. FILE

Vol 7

CONFIDENTIAL

WAR DIARY
of
204 MACHINE GUN COMPANY

From 1st Sept. 1917 to 30th Sept. 1917.

VOL. VII

Appendices.
i. Operation Orders
ii. Casualty List

WAR DIARY
INTELLIGENCE SUMMARY

(Erase heading not required.)

Army Form C. 2118.

Place	Date	Hour	Summary of Events and Information	Remarks and references to Appendices
COXYDE BAINS	Sept. 1st 1917	1st	BELGIUM SHEET II. S.E. N⁰ 2 & 3 Sections took on new harassing fire positions from 203 M.9.67 & M.27a.99 15000 rounds fired. 2/Lt. 28 N.D. FREEMAN promoted Lieut. with seniority from 31/7/17. Coomb Bay H.Q. at COXYDE BAINS, No. 6 H.Q. NIEUPORT BAINS. R.2+a 30 no	RN J
		2nd	Enemy fired some gas shells & an aeroplane came over in the night. 15000 rounds fired. Our artillery remained	RS J
		3rd	Weather very fine. Our artillery fairly active. Hostile artillery normal. Some heavy shelling around N⁰. 6. Coy. H.Q. Some gas shells were not fired on	RS J
		4th	Usual harassing fire. 10 R wounded (at night). Bombs dropped by enemy aircraft on LA PANNE.	RS J
		5th	Quiet day. Usual harassing fire. 15000 rounds fired. Enemy shelling during night. 4 5/16 h. hampered by enemy aircraft.	RS J
		6th	Enemy artillery today seemed all positions were harassing fire. COXYDE shelled by M.V. gun during day. hy.h.	RS J
		7th	Weather fine: normal harassing fire. 15000 rounds fired. Enemy M.G.s very active on our positions.	RS J
		8th	Conditions normal during the day; sudden burst of shelling 3.30 am	RS J
		9th	Enemy artillery active, some shelling round No. 6.2. Hq. working some gas shells (mustard). Our harassing fire normal.	RS J
		10th	Quiet day. Our harassing fire. Back areas bombed. 8.30-10.30 pm. Enemy bus trumpet	RS J
		11	Weather fine, normal harassing fire. COXYDE BAINS shelled by H.V. 5.9 during the night. Enemy M.G. fire	RS J

WAR DIARY
or
INTELLIGENCE SUMMARY

Army Form C. 2118.

Place	Date	Hour	Summary of Events and Information	Remarks and references to Appendices
Coy H.Q. COXYDE BAINS	12/9/17		BELGIUM 11. S.E. Adv. H.Q. heavily shelled 12 noon. New Avenue shelled at 3.0.5. A.A. platform damaged. Hanging fire in before military communications shed and lamentel	R.A.14
Adv. Coy H.Q. NIEUPORT BAINS	13/14		Heavy fire - hanging fire as stated. I.O.R. moved (all day) Relief (Coys) moved	R.B.9
	14th		Coy relieved at hanging fire trenches by 302 N.B. Coy relay completed by 12 noon. Weather milder COXYDE BAINS. Fires allowed during the evening to dry gear.	(3B) 13
	15th		Coy engaged	
	16th		Company carried out section (Section 1) training. Officers Riflemen. Brigade training ground meanwhile. No officer relieved for medical check.	R.S. 11
			Corpl. H.R.B. Duckham to U.K. on leave.	(RB)6
	17th		Coy on training on Brigade training ground. Lecture on attack with rifle by I.O.R.	R.S. 13
	18th		Met. Coy implement preparing for snow. M.G. of. Shot. J. German of No. 2 section relieved two night guns of 255 MG Coy in NIEUPORT BAINS section.	R.S.15
	19.		Weather turned to dn severe. No.1 Sect. No.2 Sect. doing the same with 1 Senior No.3 Sgt. relieved. Same sgt. taken to HEAD MK 63 Relief completed 3 am 20/9/17 attended by No.4 Sect. at 8.30 am. Enemy aeroplane bombed Coy in line. No.3 Sect. built home at actual COXYDE BAINS. Enemy carrying from aeroplane your house +800 rounds fired but without results. Harassing fire as normal. Good journey.	R.S. 15 R.S. 15

WAR DIARY
or
INTELLIGENCE SUMMARY

Army Form C. 2118.

Place	Date	Hour	Summary of Events and Information	Remarks and references to Appendices
COXYDE BAINS	23/8/17		Harassing the hostile and dug out by front line of guns. Fired two first suspected information to hy RE posters ripely to RE two rounds of punch posing steep by living slightcoms came over. Lieuts.	R.B.17
ART 40 NEUPORT BAINS	24th	2.22 am	Morning fine no hy two were activity. Enemy shelled a few at 2104a as fired	R.S.H
	25th		Lieut R DARBY & Headquarters Sh'n Enemy planes searched for our guns during morning. Fire fired rounds from our Jackdaw at enemy aircraft	R.S.L
	26th	3.30	Orders for relay wires received. B/T.G & H.2 manned all 4 wires to Relay forces issued 1 A.F were manned	R.B.17
		3.52	No relieved with time by 127 M.T.boy. A/T.G & H/T relay complete 7 Broaw remaining.	R.B.17
			Relieved COXYDE BAINS 9.30 am	R.B.17
	26th	9.30 am	Arrived NIELLES en route for GHYVELDE refilling.	
			Temporary billets assigned to Lieut R DARBY with 86 Rearstr 726 ?	S.R.K
	27th		Adv party & hulls testing Transport under P.H. & REMESURES. Spending right near WORMHOUDT. Lieut O. BENTLEY arrived + assumed command	
			Like my duties as adj.	R.B.15
CAMPAGNE 2.5 (au may) WAZE BRINK	29		Company ros horses of motors left WORMHOUDT & CAMPAGNE arriving of met REMESURES reaching new Houdt C CAMPAGNE.	O.B.15
	30		CAPT R B BUCHANAN returning to duty. Cont. E.W. STRAPP MC. returning 7 25 d 20.90 M.G CORPS CAMPAGNE (BELGIUM FRANCE SHEET 27).	P.B.15
			Company in billets training	R.B.15

Appendix I.

Operation Orders.

SECRET

Special Relief Order No 81

I. No. 204 M.G. Coy will relieve No. 203 M.G. Coy during the nights 18/19th Sept. and 19/20th Sept.

II. On the night 18/19th Sept. No. 4 Section under 2 Lt. Shaw will take over the gun emplacements R1 - R4 inclusive.

Two teams of No. 2 Section under 2 Lt. Meader will take over gun emplacement R5 & R6.

One guide per gun team will be at the Right Ration Dump (Top of Sandy Lane) M20.b.80.35. at 9.30 p.m. 18.9.17.

On the night 19/20th Sept. one gun team of No. 3 Sect. will take over R.12. M.G. emplacement. No. 1 Sect. will take over R.11. R.10. R.9 & the Lighthouse M.G. emplacements.

One gun team of No. 3 Section will take over the Station emplacements R.7 & R.8.

Lieut. Strapp will take over the charge of the "Lighthouse", R.7 & R.8, emplacements & Lt. Freeman the Coast Sections R.9 - R.12 inclusive.

III. All Trench Stores, Order Boards, Targets, Secret papers & maps & details of work in progress will be taken over & receipts given & obtained for same. Copies of these lists will be sent to Adv. Coy H.Q on the morning of the 20th inst. Particular attention will be given to the taking over of the S.O.S. or Night Lines of each gun.

IV. East of the line OOST-DONKERKE — OOST-DUNKERKE-BAINS an interval of at least 200 yards will be maintained between the Sections & transport.

V. Completion of relief will be reported to Coy H.Q — time to be stated.

VI. TRANSPORT
Three limbers will parade ready to move off at 7.0 p.m. on the night of the 18th inst.
Five limbers will parade at the same time on the night of the 19th inst.

VII. H.Q. Staff
    C.S.M.
    Pte George
    " Preston
    " McLachlan
    " Grosvenor (cook)

Ralph Darby
Lt & adjt
204 M.G. Coy.

SECRET

SPECIAL RELIEF ORDER NO. 52.

1. No 204 M.G. Coy will be relieved by the 127th M.G. Coy on the night of the 24th/25th Sept.

2. Guides will be furnished by this Company as follows
    Nos. 1-6 Gun Teams
        One guide per team at Cross Roads (M21c. 37.70) at 4.0 a.m.
    Nos. 7-12 and Lighthouse gun teams
        One guide per gun team at LAITERIE ROYALE at 9.0 p.m. These guides will report at Adv. Coy. H.Q. at 3.30 p.m.

3. TRANSPORT
    (a) Three limbers will be at Cross Roads at M21c 37.70 at 5.30 a.m.
    (b) Two limbers will be at Adv. Coy. H.Q at 4.30 a.m.
    (c) Two limbers (No.1 Section) will be at Adv. Coy. H.Q. at 5.30 a.m.
    (d) Two limbers will be at Adv. Coy. H.Q. at 6.30 p.m. for the use of Lt. Strapps gun teams.

(4) Completion of relief will be reported to Adv. Coy H.Q. by runner. On completion of relief Sections will return under Section Officers to Coy. Hqrs. COXYDE BAINS. An interval of at least 200 yds. to be maintained between sections.

(5) All Trench Stores, Secret papers & maps. S.A.A. dump Targets, A.A. positions & Fixed Drums etc. will be handed over and receipt will be obtained for same.
    All information such as Night or S.O.S. lines S.O.S. Signals, Water Supply, R.A.Ps etc. will be made known to relieving Company.

Capt. D——
Lieut.
Comdg. 204 M.G. Coy

Secret.

254th L.T. Coy. Move Orders
Ref map Hazebrouck 5a

An advance party consisting of
2/Lt. R. P. Tranter and L/Cpl Park
will move with the 9/6 Bn Leicesters.
They will report to that unit by
11.15 am 27.9.17 the Ghyvelde-Bray Dunes Rd
between the 3/1st Field Amb. & 430 Field Coy
R.E. about 400 yards S of Pont de Ghyvelde.
The above Ady Party will meet the
Coy on their arrival at the place of
debussing on Arques-Racquinghem Road
near the Windmill (under G in COMPAGNE)
Billets will be obtained on application to
Area Commandant ARQUES.

1. Transport i/c of Lieut. E. J. Symcox
accompanied by Lieut. H.W.D. Freeman
will form up (closed up) on the GHYVELDE-
LES MOERES ROAD at 8.0 am.
The Coy Transport will take up its
positions between the Transport of
the 2/6th Manc Regt and the 2/3rd Field
Amb.
Brakesmen will be detailed by the
C.S.M.

O.s. will take steps to ensure that their transport debouches on the main road in its correct position as regards other units.

Particular attention must be paid to march discipline. Steel helmets will be worn.

Brigade Group Transport will be timed not to enter WORMHOUDT before 2.30pm and must be clear of WORMHOUDT by 3.30pm.

11. The Company will move by bus from GHYVELDE to the RENESCURE Area on the 28th inst.

The Coy will parade at 9.0am on the 28th inst.

The dress will be full marching order, steel helmets will be worn, and soft Service caps will be carried in the haversack.

Strict attention must be paid to discipline and men must retain their seats when bus is on the move.

26.9.17

F. W. Strapp Lt.
Commanding 204th A.T. Coy

Appendix II

Casualty List

204 Machine Gun Coy.

Casualties for month of September 1917.

Wounded:-
46719 Sgt. Hulme (slightly) remained at duty.   5. 9. 17
86175 Pte Wallis H (")   "   "   12. 9. 17
65504 " Humphrey J (")   "   "   19. 9. 17
66572 " Rowe G. W.   24. 9. 17

Vol 8

CONFIDENTIAL.

WAR DIARY

of

204 MACHINE GUN COMPANY.

From 1st Oct. to 31st Oct. 1917.

VOL. VIII.

APPENDIX.

I. Report on operations
II. Relief Order
III. Casualty Return.

SHEET 1

Army Form C. 2118.

WAR DIARY
or
INTELLIGENCE SUMMARY.

(Erase heading not required.)

Instructions regarding War Diaries and Intelligence
Summaries are contained in F.S. Regs., Part II.
and the Staff Manual respectively. Title pages
will be prepared in manuscript.

Place	Date	Hour	Summary of Events and Information	Remarks and references to Appendices
CAMPAGNE	October 1st		Training	
	2		"	
	2	8.0 a.m.	Company entrains at ARQUES. Detrained BRANDHOEK. Billets C.H.C. 27. (Belgium) Transport move by road - whisky journey arrived in billets about midnight - raining hard. Company under canvas.	
	3		Company in Billets	
	4		"	
	5		Ordered to move forward to YPRES. 2nd Lt. P.P. Shaw & 2nd Lt. E.B. Ribon proceed to reconnoitre the line Company halts in field East of YPRES from MENIN ZONNEBEKE ROAD to POTSDAM about 5 p.m. to relieve guns of the 10th & 11th Australian Brigades. Darkness sets in. Road very bad - all mud & shell holes. No. 4 section, No. 3 section & half No. 1 section go into line remainder in reserve behind POTSDAM. Some of the Company time in devilish tanks of what there are many lying about.	
	6		The line which we are now holding has just been taken with enemy of the 4th by the Australians. Coy H.Q. move into a Pill Box it Belly	

WAR DIARY or INTELLIGENCE SUMMARY

Army Form C. 2118.

Place	Date	Hour	Summary of Events and Information	Remarks and references to Appendices
YPRES	Feb 6		2/Lt. Shaw, 2/Lt. Kiernan wounded. 1 O.R. killed & 1 O.R. wounded in Pill Box - shell burst outside during C.O.'s alone escape. Survive side slip East. No 3 return & 2 guns 9/KOYLI relieved by Australians.	
	7		Receive orders to relieve 4 guns 9/147 Bde. on our left. Also ordered to recommence barrage position near DARE CROSSING (Map GRAFENSTAFEL 1/10000) Relief arranged for morning of the 8th and coops 147 Coy Conference with DMGO midnight - relief of 147 worked out. Receive order to form barrage group 9/146 guns with 160,000 rds S.A.A. Think this impossible in view of condition of ground - not a blade of grass anywhere nor even a tree in view.	
	8	6-7	Take No 2 Pack mules away on operations. See attached report on operations.	
	9			
	10			
	11		Relieved by the 23rd Australian M.G. Coy. Company returns to huts in BRANDHOEK. The ZONNEBEKE ROAD very heavily shelled impossible to get transport up to get guns away. Transport Sgt. wounded.	
BRANDHOEK	12		Guns brought away from POTSDAM 6 a.m. having had Company collecting	

Army Form C. 2118.

WAR DIARY
or
INTELLIGENCE SUMMARY.
(Erase heading not required.)

Place	Date	Hour	Summary of Events and Information	Remarks and references to Appendices
BRANDHOEK	Oct 12		Resting & roughly cleaning stores	J
	13		Company less transport entrain at BRANDHOEK for RENESCURE area	J
			Transport move by road. Company arrive ARQUES - billeted here - 2.0 p.m.	
			still raining	
ARQUES	14		Company in billets 2 Lt C.V. Booth & 2 Lt W.B. Jones joined the Company	J
	15		Company cooking shelp out	J
	16			J
	17		Company training - weather good	J
	18			
	19			
	20		Company moved to billets in CAMPAGNE	J
	21			
	22		Company training	
	23			
	24			J
	25		Company moved to billets in MALHOVE, ARQUES	J

Army Form C. 2118.

WAR DIARY
or
INTELLIGENCE SUMMARY

(Erase heading not required.)

Place	Date	Hour	Summary of Events and Information	Remarks and references to Appendices
MALHOVE ARQUES	26		Company training	A
	27		"	A
	28		"	A
	29		Commander in Chief inspected Division. Bugo. Chronicle of the ARQUES - AIRE ROAD	A
	30		Company training	A
	31		"	A

COPY

SECRET.   199 Bde Order No. 60.

1. The following readjustment of the front line will take place tonight. Right Bde front 199 Inf Bde will become left Batt. front 7th A1 Bde.

2. The 2/5 M/C Regt will be relieved by the 25th A Bde
   the 2/6 M/C Regt.   "   "   "   26th A Bde

3. Details of relief will be arranged between O/Cs concerned.

4. (a) On relief 2/5 M/C Regt (less 1 Coy) will move on the left of the Rly. line & Batt. will be in support of 2/7 M/C Regt (Coy now on left of line standing fast.
   (b) The 2/6 M/C Regt will relieve the right support Batt. of the 147 Bde (49 Div) in the support line & will be in support of the 2/8th M/C Regt. who are relieving the front line Batt of the same Brigade.

5. The 201 M.G. Coy positions, & 199 L.T.M.B. position E of Railway line will be taken over by the MGC & 7th A.L.T.M.B. respectively. Details to be arranged between O/Cs concerned.

6. Relief to be complete by 5 a.m. 7th inst.

7. Ack.

(Sgd) C.H. Fox Capt
For Bde Major
199 Inf. Bde.

Report on Operations October 9th 1917

Situation — The disposition of the guns of this Company on the day previous to the attack was 4 guns with the 2/7th Manchester Regt on the right of the Brigade front. 12 guns at Coy. H.Q. (4 of these had just been withdrawn from the line owing to the side slip of the division. 4 were pending to relieve 4 guns of the 147 M.G. Coy.

At 6.30 a.m. on the 8th inst. No. 2 Section under 2 Lt Kensington with 8 pack animals left Coy Hqrs. for Barrage positions.

At about 9.0 a.m. a runner returned from this Section with the news that it was impossible to proceed with the pack animals owing to the condition of the ground along the tape track. — an attempt was being made to get along the Railway track. This latter was also found to be impossible and the loads had to be dumped and manhandled. Under these conditions it was realised that it was an impossible task to push up 12 guns with the necessary appliances and S.A.A. It was decided therefore to get an additional 6 guns up and thus make a 10 gun group.

Owing to the arrangements made by division regarding an extra days rations to be carried on the men, my T.O. did not receive instructions regarding additional pack animals, limbers, etc. (copy of orders attached) until 4.30. a.m. at Coy H.Q POTSDAM from where he had to return to BRANDHOEK.

160 Boxes of S.A.A. were drawn from the Divisional Dump at POTIJZE but owing to blocks in traffic etc this did not arrive till well on in afternoon at Coy H.Q.

By this time 2 Lt. Mander went off with a section with 2 guns and 50 belt boxes. These

(2)

were taken on pack animals to the Railway Bridge on the ZONNEBEKE ROAD where they were dumped. It was proposed to "manhandle" from this point in future. It was raining hard, the condition of the ground was appalling and the light was bad - failing quickly.

2 Lt. E.B. Ritson at about 4.30 set off with a party with S.A.A. boxes on pack animals. This party with two others succeeded in dumping about 80 boxes S.A.A. at the Railway Bridge.

With the exception of 4 H.Q. staff all men were now out on their way to the barrage positions and "in the blue" so far as my knowledge went.

I remained at rear Company H.Q. until 4.0. a.m. on the morning of the 9th so that I could be available to collect any runners returning from these parties.

At 5.20 a.m. I reached 198 B.H.Q. LEVI COTTAGES. No runner had arrived there from the gun positions.

At about 8.0. a.m. a sergeant & several men arrived at LEVI COTTAGES with 2 guns and a few (probably 15) belt boxes. They were in an exhausted condition. Runners which I had sent forward had not yet returned. I could only now presume that in all there were 7 gunners at the barrage positions. (1 having been reported lost with a mule.)

At about noon ten men arrived at Ad. Coy. H.Q. from the rear H.Q. having returned there after being out all night. These with 5 others I sent to barrage positions with belt boxes, a gun and a tripod.

(3)

The runners had now returned from 2 Lt Wallsgrove who reported that owing to the attacking infantry failing to arrive on the tape line at ZERO hour and the infantry of the garrison having evacuated the trenches he had only withdrawn his guns which were already in the line to positions just in front of the tape line in case of anything happening. Later when the attacking infantry had dribbled forward never having assembled on the tape line, he occupied positions previously chosen from whence he could hold the original front line and at the same time fire on his S.O.S. Lines. His section had suffered very heavy casualties & 2 bipods had been blown up.

At 5.0 p.m. in the evening the S.O.S signal was fired on. Shortly after this parties of our infantry were seen to be retiring on our positions about the R in HAMBURG. All available machine gunners were turned out & those with revolvers armed with Boche rifles & bayonets. The infantry which were retiring through our positions were held up and strong points – four in all – organised around the guns. A Lewis gunner with his gun & some S.A.A. was also scooped in. For this work I consider 2 Lt Wallsgrove & 2 Lt Kenchington deserve great credit as probably a further retirement might have matured.

By 5.30 p.m. in the evening I had managed to get something like 30 boxes of S.A.A. formed into a dump at LEVI COTTAGES and more belt boxes sent into the line.

(4)

It was now quite evident that the other guns had not reached their positions. Word came to hand that 2 Lt Ritson was missing & 2 Lt Maunder wounded.

During the day of the 10th inst. 2 guns which were at Levi Cottages were mounted against enemy aeroplanes which had been busy at low altitudes.

The OC. 23rd Australian M.G. Coy arrived to take over barrage positions. The relief was arranged to take place early the following morning (11th). In the meantime Officers of the 11th Australian M.G.Coy. had arranged to take over gun positions then being held by 2 Lt. Wellgrove.

The total casualties sustained during the operations and their preparation amounted to 5 officers (wounded) 7 O.R. (killed) 20 (wounded) 1 O.R. (sick).

That the barrage was a failure so far as my group went there was no doubt. In my opinion the reasons for this were:-

    1. Lack of time for preparation
    2. Opposing conditions (climatic & state of ground)
    3. Loss of control by officers
    4. Insufficient personnel
    5. Exhausted condition of the men
    6. Transport much too far away

(BRANDHOEK)

(Sgd) B. Buchanan
Captain
Comdg. 2nd M.G. Coy.

13 Oct. 1917.

Reinforcements
1st Oct. to 31 Oct. 1917.

Officers   Lieut C. Saxby. 2nd in Command.
              2 Lieut H.B. Jones
              2 Lieut. C. V. Booth
              2 Lieut R.P. Shaw
              2 Lieut. A.C. Soward.

Rank O.R. 33.

Casualties
1st Oct '17 to 31st Oct '17

Officers.
    4 wounded
    1 Missing

O.R.
    9 killed
  20~~30~~ wounded.

CONFIDENTIAL

WAR DIARY

of

204 MACHINE GUN COMPANY

From 1st Nov. 1917 to 30th Nov. 1917

Vol. IX.

Appendix

Casualty Return.

WAR DIARY
INTELLIGENCE SUMMARY

Sheet I.   November 1917   Army Form C. 2118.

No 204 Machine Gun Company

Place	Date Novr.	Hour	Summary of Events and Information	Remarks and references to Appendices
Staples	1st		Company moved to billets at Staples. 2/Lt MANDER joined the Coy.	2 W.D.h
	2nd		Company training	2 W.D.h
	3rd		— do —	2 W.D.h
	4th		— do —	2 W.D.h
	5th		— do —	2 W.D.h
	6th		— do —	2 W.D.h
	7th		— do —	2 W.D.h
			Capt. Buchanan proceeded to Camiers. Lieut Darby took over Command of Company. Lieut Straff reported in Command.	2 W.D.h
	8th		Company training. Transport proceeded to Eecke by road under Bde pack arrangements.	2 W.D.h
Westoutre	9th		Company moved by rail from EBBLINGHEM to WESTOUTRE and were joined there by the transport.	2 W.D.h
SWAN AREA YPRES	10th		Company marched with transport to camp at Devon area YPRES	2 W.D.h
	11th	1.0 a.m	Company moved up into Barrage Line positions and relieved 3rd Australian M.G. Coy. 16 guns.	2 W.D.h
	12th		No 2 & 4 Sections relieved by two sections of 203 Coy. (A Battery) 8 guns. Two O.R. wounded. Both subsequently evacuated.	2 W.D.h
	13th		Clearing up. Weather fine. Rear Head quarters established in Camp near Chateau Belge evacuated by 3rd A. M. G. Coy.	2 W.D.h

Sheet II. November 1917

Army Form C. 2118.

WAR DIARY
or
INTELLIGENCE SUMMARY

(Erase heading not required.)

No. 204 Machine Gun Company

Place	Date Nov.	Hour	Summary of Events and Information	Remarks and references to Appendices
Swan Area YPRES	14th		Settling down in new Camp. Sorting stores. A.P.S. Great feat. Guns carried out Indirect fire on enemy roads & communications. Fired 11000 rounds in reply to S.O.S.	7.10 W.D.
	15th		Preparing to relieve Sections by Sections at Barrage positions (C.T.A.) Rear Headquarters. Fired 14,500 rounds in reply to MANDER & two S.R.	2.10 W.D.
	16th		Relief carried out in early morning. 2/Lt. Jones wounded but remained at duty. One Trigger destroyed by shell fire. Guns carried out several indirect fire from Barrage positions cleaning up. Guns carried	2.10 W.D.
	17th		Men relieved from Barrage positions. Communications out. Indirect fire on enemy positions not on Barrage Wd. Indirect	2.10 W.D.
	18th		Cleaning limbers by sections. Communications by Barrage fire. Indirect fire on Enemy Stations & Communications. Indirect fire by Barrage fire as usual.	4.10 W.D.
	19th		Company training. Two Sections do	4.10 W.D.
	20th		do	2.10 W.D.
	21st		Inter Company relief at Barrage positions in early morning. 9th Company left at A.B.S. with last pack mg pack mg (relieve last.) Moral Indirect fire on enemy positions & communications.	4.10 W.D.
	22nd		Men relieved from Barrage positions cleaning up. Indirect fire by Barrage fire as usual.	4.10 W.D.

WAR DIARY or INTELLIGENCE SUMMARY

Army Form C. 2118.

Sheet III   November 1917

No 204 Machine Gun Company

Place	Date Nov	Hour	Summary of Events and Information	Remarks and references to Appendices
Staplefords and Ypres	23rd		Company eight guns on Barrage work relieved by four guns 1st New Zealand M.G. Coy. in early morning and N.C.O. Large 2/ men sent up to assist in carrying out guns 2. 2 O.R. wounded & evacuated.	7.W.J.L.
SWAN AREA YPRES	24		Cleaning up. Packing limbers - getting ready to move to BERTHEN AREA & billets in Berthen	7.W.J.L.
BERTHEN AREA	25		Company moved with 202 Company M.G.C. to billets in Berthen area.	7.W.J.L.
STAPLES (Sub area)	26		Coy moved to billets in Staples sub area. (near Caestre)	7.W.J.L.
	27		Cleaning and checking stores	7.W.J.L.
	28		Cleaning limbers and checking belts & boxes. 2 O.R. reinforcements reported	7.W.J.L.
	29		Company training. 19 O.R. re-inforcements reported.	7.W.J.L.
	30		Company training	7.W.J.L.

Appendix

Casualty Return.

Nov. 1917.

Officers.   2Lt. Mander R.P. wounded 16.11.17.

O.Rs.   7 wounded.

CONFIDENTIAL

WAR DIARY
— of —
204 MACHINE GUN COMPANY.

From 1st Dec' 1917 to 31st Dec' 1917.

Vol. X

Appendix
i. Programme of Work
ii. Casualty Return.

WAR DIARY

Sheet 1.

Army Form C. 2118.

INTELLIGENCE SUMMARY. December 1917.

204 Machine Gun Company

Place	Date	Hour	Summary of Events and Information	Remarks and references to Appendices
	1917			
ST.SYLVESTRE CAPPEL	Dec 1.		Company Training	
	2		Do	
	3		Do	
	4		Do	
	5		Do	
	6		Capt R.B Buchanan returned from Course at CAMIERS	
	7		Company Training	
	8		Do	
	9		Do	
	10		Do	
	11		No.3 v. No 2 Section Football Final. No.3 Section won 3-1	
	12		Company Training	
	13		Do	
	14		As Programme of work	
	15		Do	

Army Form C. 2118.

Sheet 2.

December 1917

WAR DIARY
or
INTELLIGENCE SUMMARY.

(Erase heading not required.)

204 Machine Gun Coy

Place	Date	Hour	Summary of Events and Information	Remarks and references to Appendices
ST SYLVESTRE CAPPEL	1917 Dec 16		32 men were attached from Brigade. They should prove useful.	
	17		Range commenced near HAZEBROUCK on the HAZEBROUCK – ST SYLVESTRE CAPPEL Road. Digging is very difficult owing to the frozen state of the ground	
	18		Company training & digging	
	19		Christmas celebrations held. Freezing hard. Everything went well	
	20		Range digging almost impossible, the ground is so hard. Concert held in the evening in a large hut/vaviment	
	21 31		Company training and building range.	

APPENDIX

Programme of Work 10-12-17 to 17-12-17

Day	Sect	7.0 – 9.15	9.15 – 9.45	9.45 – 10.15	10.15 – 10.45	11.0 – 12.30	Sundry
Monday	1, 2, 3, 4		Baths		(and Lectures on Barrage Drill)		
Tuesday	1	A.A. Shooting	Pack Transport			Barrage Drill	All Range Takers 9.15 – 10.15
	2	Range Cards	L.A. + Mech.	A.A. Shooting			
	3, 4	Close Order Drill	Bombing	Close Order Drill			
			A.A. Shooting				
Wednesday	1, 2	Barrage Drill		Elementary Drills		Lecture "Machine Gunners" by C.O.	Lecture All NCOs Direct overhead Fire by C.O.
	3, 4						
Thursday	1, 2	Company Close Order Drill	Tpt Traverse Marching	Care of guns in severe weather + Equipment		Barrage Drill	
	3, 4		Anti-aircraft sights			Pack Transport Barrage Drill	
Friday	1, 2	Route March with loads	⟶	Lecture by C.O. "Elementary Tactics" – Inspections		Lecture by C.O.	Lecture All NCOs – The effect of atmospheric conditions on M.G. Fire by C.O. 2.0 – 3.30 pm
	3, 4						
Saturday	1, 2	Range Cards Revolver Practice	Gas Training	Direct O.F. Gas Training	Direct O.F.	Barrage Drill	
	3	A.A. Shooting	Barrage Drill	Barrage Drill		Pack Transport	
	4	Direct O.F.	Pack Transport			Barrage Drill	

Programme of Work.

Dec. 1917		7.0	9.15 – 9.45	9.45 – 10.15	10.15 – 10.45	11.0 – 12.30	2.15 p.m.
Monday 17th	1	A	March to Range	Building Range. Parade 8.30 a.m.			Lecture all NCOs "Effects of Atmosphere on M.G. Fire."
	2			Ind. rts. of Targets Company loads	D.O.Z. Rifle Range	Rifle Range Ind. & D.O.Z.	
	3				O.A. Shooting Pack Transport		
	4		Close Order Drill	Tap Traverse		P.T	
Tuesday 18th	1		Programme as for 2 & 3 Monday.				Lecture for Officers "M.G. Tactics"
	2		Building Range				
	3		Programme as for 4 Monday				
	4		Programme as for 2 & 3 Monday				
Wednesday 19th							
Thursday 20th	1		Close Order Drill Tap Traverse	Pack Transport	Elementary Tactics		Officers Tactical Ride
	2		Close Order Drill	Building Range			
	3		Another Prac. O.A. Shooting	Saluting	Elementary Tactics		
	4						
Friday 21st	1		Barrage Drill (keeping Guns by compass)	Saluting Bombing	Elementary Tactics		Lecture all NCOs "M.G. Tactics"
	2						
	3		Close Order Drill	A.A. Shooting Range Cards			
	4			Building Range			
Saturday 22nd	1		Saluting	A.A. Shooting	Range Cards	Elementary Tactics	
	2		Barrage Drill (keeping Guns by compass)	Bombing			
	3			Saluting			
	4						

Casualty Return

December 1917.

NIL

Confidential

War Diary
of
204. Machine Gun Company

1st Jany. 1918 to 31st Jany. 1918

Vol. XI.

Appendices
① Movements
② Relief Orders

Army Form C. 2118.

WAR DIARY
or
INTELLIGENCE SUMMARY.

204 Shropshire Spure Coy

(Erase heading not required.)

Place	Date	Hour	Summary of Events and Information	Remarks and references to Appendices
ST SYLVESTRE CAPPEL	Jan 1918 1		Company Training	
	2		"	
	3		"	
	4		"	
	5		"	
	6		"	
	7		"	
	8		"	
	9		"	
	10		Packing limbers and checking and collecting area stores	
	11		Transport moved for CANAL AREA YPRES (two days trek)	
	12		Company moved by lorries to POTIJZE	
			Company having + preparing for half of company to go into the line	
	13		Half Company with eight guns relieved 8 guns of 176th Company in the line	

Army Form C. 2118.

WAR DIARY
or
INTELLIGENCE SUMMARY. 204 Machine Gun Coy

(Erase heading not required.)

Instructions regarding War Diaries and Intelligence Summaries are contained in F. S. Regs., Part II. and the Staff Manual respectively. Title pages will be prepared in manuscript.

Place	Date	Hour	Summary of Events and Information	Remarks and references to Appendices
	Jan 1918 14		Company training for half company not in the line	
	15		Moved to Burgomaso in CHIPS AREA H24 a 15.90.	
	16		Company training and improving and cleaning Camp. Heavy rain. Improving Camp & Transport lines	
	17		Do	
	18		Do	
	19		Inner company relief in line. 3th section relieved 2nd section	
	20		Cleaning up by men returning from line	
	21		Building fresh latrines, cookhouse areas etc. Menning Camp putting down duckpaths & disc boards	
	22		Do	
	23		Do	
	24		Do	
	25		Capt Buchanan proceeded on leave. Lt. C. Jacoby assumed command. 2Lt. Wallgrove 2nd in Command	
	26		Inter company relief 1st Section relieved 4th section	

Army Form C. 2118.

WAR DIARY 204 Machine Gun Coy
or
INTELLIGENCE SUMMARY.

(Erase heading not required.)

Instructions regarding War Diaries and Intelligence Summaries are contained in F. S. Regs., Part II. and the Staff Manual respectively. Title pages will be prepared in manuscript.

Place	Date	Hour	Summary of Events and Information	Remarks and references to Appendices
	Jan 1918 26		Cleaning up by men returned from line	
	27		Company having Camp fatigues	
	28		Company having new Emplacements tobelieve made on the line	
	29		Do	
	30		New emplacements in line required by half company July	
	31		Inter company relief in line. No 3 my section relieved 2nd section	

Appendix

Movements & Relief Orders

SECRET.   204 M.G. Coy.   Copy No 5
                         Movement Order No.
        Sheets 27 & 28   Part I.

Move   The 204 M.G. Coy (see part II for transport) will
                move by bus to POTIZZE on the 11th inst.
                Embussing point Q.31.b.3.4. at 8.45 a.m.
                Column moves 9.30 a.m.

Billeting   A billeting party consisting of 2/Lt. H. Kenchington
Party.   Cpl. W. Storey & L/Cpl J. Sharpe will report at the
                Staff Captains' Office at 7.45 a.m. on the 10th inst.
                Rations for the 10th & 11th will be carried (except
                by man returning) This party will proceed
                then to BELGIAN CHATEAU to find location of
                Q.M. Stores. One of the party will then return to
                the Company in order to guide lorry. The remainder
                of the party will proceed to Area Commandant
                POTIZZE area (I.4.c.6.5.) for accomodation for Coy.
                arriving on the 11th inst. One of this party must meet
                the stores lorry at Q.M. Stores at BELGIAN CHATEAU in
                order to guide it on to POTIZZE

Additional   One motor lorry is allotted to this Company for
Transport   extra stores. A guide for this lorry will report
                to the Staff Captains office CAESTRE at 6.45 a.m. on
                the 11th inst. All stores for this lorry must be
                at Q.M. Stores by 7.15 a.m.. The lorry will then
                proceed to Q.M. Stores at BELGIAN CHATEAU & then on
                to POTIZZE .

Rations   Rations for consumption on the 11th inst. will
                be carried by sections.
                Rations for consumption on the 12th inst will
                be delivered by train waggons to Q.M. Stores.
                They must then be sent on to POTIZZE by our
                own transport

Part II.

Mode — The transport will move at 8.30 a.m. on the 10th inst. according to table.

	From.	To.	Route	Remarks
10th.	CAESTRE	WIPPENHOEK	CAESTRE – GODEWAERSVELDE – ABEELE	Accompanying Transport 199 Bde group
11th.	WIPPENHOEK	H.17c 5/4 Lines 146 M.G.C.	No restrictions	
13th.	H.17c 5/4	H.18c 4/3 Lines 254 M.G.C.	"	

Rations — Rations for the 10th & 11th will be carried on the limbers. The Mess wagon which will accompany the transport will draw rations for the 12th inst. R.P. to be notified later.

Packs & Blankets — The packs & blankets of the transport & brakesmen will be carried on the limbers & not rolled with sections.

Guide (1st day only) — A mounted party will report at least 3 hours before arrival of the transport to Lt. Col. MULLINER Area Commandant WIPPENHOEK.

Brakesmen — The following will be brakesmen on "C" & H.Q. limbers.

　　L/Cpl. Slater G.
　　Pte. Allen J.W.
　　Pte. Barrett B.A. TURNER
　　Pte. Smith H.
　　Pte. Burkes. R.

Sections will find brakesmen for "A" & "B" limbers.

Attached Wagon — The Baggage wagon of the L.T.M.B. will join the column at point Q.25.c.0.1.

　　　　　　　　　　　(Signed) R. B. Buchanan
Coy. H.Q. 9.10.17.　　　　　　　　　　Capt.
　　　　　　　　　　　Comdg. 204 M.G. Coy.

　　　　　Copy No. 1. C.O.
　　　　　　"　2. 2nd in Command
　　　　　　"　3. T.O.
　　　　　　"　4. Billeting officer
　　　　　　"　5. War Diary
　　　　　　"　6. Do
　　　　　　"　7. Office

Operation Orders by Capt R.B.Buchanan
 Cmdg. 20th M.G. Coy.

The 20th M.G. Coy will relieve the 146 M.G.Coy
in the line on 13th inst.
Four guns in the front line position
2 Right guns at Barrage position +
one A.A. gun

S.O.S. up to 12 noon on the 15th will be rifle
grenade signal bursting into 2 red
stars + 2 white stars simultaneously
S.O.S. after 12 noon 15th inst. will be rifle
grenade signal bursting into three
coloured hanging stars red over green
over yellow

Pte Farmer will be at C.H.Q. as runner
Two signallers go to C.H.Q. + take 2
telephones
Reports will be sent to C.H.Q. in accordance
with procedure of preceding Company.

Dumps S.A.A MOULIN FARM & GARTER POINT.
R.E. material YORKSHIRE DUMP

Rations + water for Barrage guns + A.A gun
will be carried by limber to GASOMETER
ZONNEBEKE + from there by carrying party
to Section HQ.
Rations for front line guns will be

(2)

carried by transport pack mules to a
point — where they will be met by
ration party from C.H.Q.
Ration will be at meeting place by 5·0 am.
Medical Aid Post will be at Right Batt'n
HQ. (Tit. J.5
(D22 c 10. Left Batt'n Aid Post. Soda
   Water factory)
Adv C.H.Q. at MOLENAARELSHOEK
Relief complete will be notified by to
C.H.Q. by "HAPPY"
Eight spare men from No 2 Section will
be at C.H.Q. as working party & ration
carriers.
Three gun teams of No 1 Section under
Lt Brooks will relieve the 2 right
guns of B. Battery & the R.A. gun.
Lumber will be packed & teams ready
to start at 12 noon.
Guide will meet this Party at DEVILS CROSSING
at 1 pm to guide them to Section H.Q.
Spare men of No 1 Section will be at rear
Coy. H.Q. & will act as ration carrying
party.
No 2 Section under Lt W.D Jones will, with
Sgt Ryder & 1 gun team of No 1 Section
will relieve the four guns in the front line.
Guns & gear will be carried on pack mules
Mules will be at LANCER CAMP by 12·30 pm.
Their teams will be ready to start at
1·30 pm

(3)

Guides will meet at E.116 CROSSING at 12.30 pm to guide teams to E.116 loop hole. 4 + 14 Lewis Gun per gun will be handed over by Canning teams.

Each team will take spare condenser, spare barrel, spare port box, thermometer, oil, rag, oil can case.

Teams will parade in fighting order – Greatcoat rolled, sandbag round legs in place of puttees. Puttees to be left in packs. Trench foot powder tins will be taken also cleaning materials. Every man will carry 2 dry pairs of socks in his haversack.

Packs will be labelled & left in Coy. Stores.

C.H.Q.
12.1.18.

Gicby(?)
a/y

SECRET   COPY No. 8

204 Machine Gun Coy.
RELIEF ORDERS.

Jan. 18. 1918.

1. No. 1 & 2 Sections will be relieved by No. 3 & 4 Sections respectively on the 19th inst.

2. Guides will meet No. 3 Sect. (less 1 team) at the GASOMETER at 12.0. noon. Guides will meet No. 4 Section plus 1 team of No. 3 Sect. at Coy. HQ. at 4.0 pm. The Guides from No. 2 Sect. will be taken from the reserve men at Coy. HQ. to guide the incoming teams direct to their positions. One guide will also be provided for H.Q. staff.

3. The gun team from No. 3 sect. which accompanies No. 4 Sect. must have a sergeant in addition to complete team.

4. No. 3 Sec. will arrange to relieve the runner at the RELAY POST at DEVILS CROSSING (This man is rationed by the Company at this Post.)

5. Everything except guns & cases, condensers, spare parts boxes, spare barrels & clinometers will be handed over. Trench stores will be handed over in the usual way & receipts taken. Copies of maps, charts, fire orders etc will be handed over.

6. The whole of the Coy. H.Q. staff except signallers will be relieved. Pte. Farmer will remain for one day as runner to 2nd in Command.

7. The relieving teams etc. will bring in with them rations & water for consumption on the 20th inst, including one "Tommy's Cooker" per team.

8. Each man coming into the line must be in possession of 3 pairs of socks. Section officers will render a return to A/Coy. H.Q. certifying that each man of their section has this number with him in the line on 20th inst.

9. All dugouts & positions will be handed over in a clean & sanitary condition. Certificates to this effect are to be sent to A/Coy. H.Q. by evening of 20th inst.

10. Completion of relief will be reported by code word "SUNSHINE"

11. A limber will meet the teams relieved at FROST HOUSE for No.1 Sect. at 1.20 pm. for No.2 Sect. at 7.0 pm.

12. Acknowledge

        (Sgd) R.B. Buchanan
                     Capt.

Copy No. 1   O.C. No 1 Sect.
        2   O.C. No 2 Sect.
        3   O.C. No 3 Sect.
        4   O.C. No 4 Sect.
        5   2nd in Command
        6   CO
        7   T.O.
        8 } War Diary
        9 }
       10   File

Advance
Coy H.Q.
Jan. 18. 1918.

SECRET   204th Machine Gun Coy.   Copy No. 7

RELIEF ORDERS.

Jan. 24. 1918.

1. No. 3 & 4 Sections will be relieved by Nos. 1 & 2 Sections respectively on the 25th inst.

2. No guides will be required by No. 2 section. This section (less 1 team) will pass the GASOMETER at 12.0. noon.
   No. 1 Section will send 1 guide for each gun position to ADV. COY. H.Q. at 4.15 p.m.

3. One gun team of 4 men & 1 gun commander of No. 2 Section will accompany No. 1 section to ADV. COY. H.Q. Sgt. Redhead will be attached to this team.

4. No. 1 Section must take 8 men as reserve to live at ADV. COY. H.Q. They will relieve 8 men of No. 4 section. Each gun team going up to their position should take 2 of these men who will return to ADV. COY. H.Q.

5. Two signallers will relieve the signallers 203 M.G. Coy. at ADV. COY. H.Q. They will take in with them 1 Fullerphone + 1 'D3'.

6. The relieving teams will take in with them rations & water for the 26th inst. Each team will take 1 'Tommys Cooker'.

7. Everything except guns & cases, condensers, spare parts boxes, spare barrels & clinometers will be handed over in the usual way & receipt taken. Copies of maps, charts, fire orders etc. will be handed over also all new gun position sites for gun positions & work in hand.

8. All dug outs & positions will be handed over in a clean & sanitary condition. Certificates to this effect are to be sent to A/COY. H.Q. by the evening of the 26th inst.

9. The limber will wait near the GASOMETER for the completion of the 2 & 3 section relief. O.C. No. 3 section will arrange to get his gear away as quickly as possible. A limber will be at ZONNEBEKE CHURCH at 5.45 p.m. for No. 4 Section.

10. Every man going into the line must be in possession of 3 pairs of dry socks & a tin full of talc powder. A certificate will be sent to A/Coy. H.Q. to this effect by evening of 26th inst.

11. No. 2 section will arrange for the relief of the runner at the RELAY POST DEVILS CROSSING.

12. Acknowledge.

R. B. Buchanan
CAPTAIN
COMDG. No. 204 COY.

204 M.G. Coy. H.Q.
Jan. 24. 1918.

Copy No. 1   O.C. No. 1 Section
  "   " 2   "   " 2   "
  "   " 3   "   " 3   "
  "   " 4   "   " 4   "
  "   " 5   2nd in Command
  "   " 6   T.O.
  "   " 7 } War Diary
  "   " 8 }
  "   " 9   File
  "   " 10 Spare

Secret

204 MACHINE GUN COMPANY.
RELIEF ORDERS

Copy 7

Jan. 30. 1918.

1. No. 1 & 2 Sections will be relieved by No. 3 & 4 sections respectively on the 31st inst.
2. Guides will meet No. 4 section at the GASOMETER at 4.30 p.m.
   No 1 section will send 1 guide for each gun position to ADV. COY. H.Q. at 4.15 p.m.
3. One N.C.O. & one O.R. of No. 4 section will be attached to C.H.Q.
4. No. 3 section must take 8 men as reserve to live at ADV. COY. H.Q. They will relieve 8 men of No. 2 section. Each gun team going up to their position should take 2 of these men who will return to ADV. COY. H.Q.
5. Two signallers of 203 M.G. Coy. will relieve the signallers at ADV. COY. H.Q.
6. The relieving teams will take in with them rations & water for the first of February. Each team will take 1 Tommy cooker.
7. Everything except guns & cases, condensers, spare part boxes, spare barrels & clinometers will be handed over. Also all new gun position sites for gun positions & work in hand.
8. All dug outs & positions will be handed over in a clean & sanitary condition. Certificates to this effect are to be sent to M/Coy H.Q. by the evening of the 1st Feb.
9. The limber will wait near the GASOMETER for the completion of the 2 & 4 section relief. O.C. No. 2 section will arrange to get his gear away as quickly as possible. A limber will be at ZONNEBEKE CHURCH at 6.15 p.m. for No. 1 Section.
10. Every man going into the line must be in possession of 3 pairs of dry socks & a tin full of talc powder. A certificate will be sent to M/Coy H.Q. to this effect by evening of 1st Feb.
11. No. 4 section will arrange for the relief of the runner at the RELAY POST DEVILS CROSSING
12. Acknowledge.

204 M.G. Coy. H.Q.
  Jan. 30. '18

   Copy No. 1 O.C. No. 1 Section
     "   " 2 "   " 2   "
     "   " 3 "   " 3   "
     "   " 4 "   " 4   "
     "   " 5 2nd in Command
     "   " 6 T.O.
     "   " 7 War Diary
     "   " 8 File
     "   " 9 Spare

COMDG. No. 204 M.G. COY.

Confidential

War Diary
of
204 Machine Gun Company

From 1st Feb. 1918 To 26th Feb. 1918

Vol. XII

Appendices:—
I. Reliefs & Move Orders.

Army Form C. 2118.

P.1.

WAR DIARY
or
INTELLIGENCE SUMMARY.   204 Machine Gun Coy

(Erase heading not required.)

Instructions regarding War Diaries and Intelligence Summaries are contained in F. S. Regs., Part II. and the Staff Manual respectively. Title pages will be prepared in manuscript.

Place	Date	Hour	Summary of Events and Information	Remarks and references to Appendices
CANAL AREA H2a.05.90.	Feb 1918 1		Test carried out with Vickers guns firing 20,000 without check cover - result guns overheated very quickly. 1 & 2 Sections at REAR BILLETS. 3 & 4 Sections in LINE.	
	2		2nd Lt R.P. Shaw returns from leave O.K. Lt. C.H. Booth proceeds on leave. Company at both billets employed in improving camp & transport lines.	
	3		2nd Lt Shaw proceeds to Labour H.Q. in LILLE to help 2nd Kensingtons owing to great difficulty in getting recruit guns in forward positions between lights. Position 81.4 improved & cleared. Friendly Coy on left took outer added. Gauge in left section found to be useless in frosty weather owing to rime - gauge taken out.	
	4		Special orders for 81.4 made out. Line circuits so to whether all the forward billets 81,182, was covered - men sent out from each position along line of eight of guns and it was made certain that all ground was properly swept. Company still employed in rear billets in making improvements especially to standings at transport.	

(A7883) Wt W809/M1672 550,000 4/17 Sch. 52a. Forms/C/2118/14

Army Form C. 2118.

WAR DIARY
or
INTELLIGENCE SUMMARY.

(Erase heading not required.)

204 Machine Gun Coy

Instructions regarding War Diaries and Intelligence Summaries are contained in F. S. Regs., Part II. and the Staff Manual respectively. Title pages will be prepared in manuscript.

Place	Date 1918	Hour	Summary of Events and Information	Remarks and references to Appendices
	Feb 5		Received Rations for "B" Battery made up to 1,200 & dumps formed at D.22.d.9.6. 50 galls. of water added & dumps marked with board. JM	
	6		261.14.B Gave relieved 2.H.A.B. forward at "B" Battery were all attached who reported sick this morning. Emplacement at 187 rounds to everyone field artillery. JM	
	7		No 3. Section relieved by 4 guns 1st N.Z. M.G. Coy. 1st N.Z. M.G. Coy relief completed without a casualty in RELIEF ORDER. JM	SEE RELIEF ORDER
	8		2 guns at "B" Battery relieved by rng 1st M.G. Coy & 3 section by 245th M.G. Coy. Casualties Nil. See whole Company in REAR BILLETS.	SEE 14/2/18 RELIEF ORDER
	9		2 huts obtained from Area Commandant to provide accommodation for 211 R.G. Saward proceeds to SENOCK CAMP PROVOST MRSP to recommence gun for having purpose also to fix up TUBS. Coy. engaged in removing blankets and from Laundry + clothing. O.C. undertook	
	10		makes his first inspection everywhere employed with exception of armourer JM	
	11		Day again broken up with cleaning Armourer returning to duty JM Company moves to SCHOOL CAMP. Day fine Capt R.B. Buchanan	

WAR DIARY
or
INTELLIGENCE SUMMARY.
(Erase heading not required.)

Army Form C. 2118.

p. 3   204 Meadow Gun Coy

Place	Date	Hour	Summary of Events and Information	Remarks and references to Appendices
	Feb 1918 11		returns from leave U.K. Coy in huts	
	12		N.C.Os proceed on leave. Company employed in clearing up. Company fell ready for interior training.	
	13		Cleaning fires on short range TM 2 O/Rs Jones two deserters from 26th Manchester Brought on escort to U.K. 7 men attached from 26th Manchester Regt. return to Unit from followers when for O/R	
	14		Intense training weather wet Sgt Crumpton & Cpl Harry proceed to CHINNERS to attend M.G. Course Pumber Bowley supposed for the M.G.Cps. Supplies & Praput return to Base Army supposed for the M.G.Cps. Company fire on "B" Range TUNNELLING CAMP 1 R.O. & 3 men proceed on leave to U.K. Cpl.	
	15			
	16		Day spent in preparing for move & cleaning up generally Brigadier very pleased with transport on Brigadier today Cpl. Company move by train into new area FRANCVILLE arriving at 2.30 am 18/2/18 Cpl.	Sgt. Mc. [?] [?] No. 2 [?]
	17			
	18		Company comfortably settled Inspection parade & fatigues only	

Army Form C. 2118.

WAR DIARY
or
INTELLIGENCE SUMMARY.

20th Machine Gun Coy

(Erase heading not required.)

Place	Date	Hour	Summary of Events and Information	Remarks and references to Appendices
	1918 Feb			
	18		Country reconnoitred for parade ground. QUARRY AREA discovered. A splendid place for indirect overhead & firing fire.	
	19		Direct overhead firing & Barrage Drill in QUARRY AREA. A beautiful day. P.M.	
	20		Company parade again in QUARRY AREA. A much colder day but fine. Lieut C.L. Booth returned from leave U.K. Received O.W. Handy reports from Base B.f.m.	
	21		A demonstration of Barrage in QUARRY excellent results. Many opportunities required for such work. Battalion worked in regard to own cooperation in tactical exercises, weather fine P.M. Weather wet. Tactical exercises carried out under either officers. Ground to be used for 2/6th Manchester's scheme reconnoitred & practice by infantry watched P.m.	
	22			
	23		Tactical exercises carried out in conjunction with 2/6 Manchester. Regt weather fine P.m.	
	24		Company moves from FRAMERVILLE to camp 1½ miles west of	

Army Form C. 2118.

WAR DIARY
or
INTELLIGENCE SUMMARY.

(Erase heading not required.)

204 Machine Gun Coy   p.5

Instructions regarding War Diaries and Intelligence Summaries are contained in F. S. Regs., Part II. and the Staff Manual respectively. Title pages will be prepared in manuscript.

Place	Date	Hour	Summary of Events and Information	Remarks and references to Appendices
	1918 Feb 24		At VILLERS CARBONNEL. Inspection by G.O.C. Company congratulated on smart appearance. Special orders issued.	
	25		Company moved into IRRIGILES. Sector of line to be taken over reconnoitered. Very wet during morning but fine afternoon & evening.	
	26		Three sections in line. Nos 1,2 & 4. No 3 with guns in reserve + No 2 on Anti-Aircraft work at HANCOURT. 12,000 rounds fired by sections in line on harassing targets and on S.O.S. going up on LEFT FRONT.	
	27		Dull day. 3000 rounds fired on sunken road behind enemy line.	
	28		Rather fine. Hostile shelling around Coy. H.Q. 3000 rounds fired by FERVAQUE guns.	

Appendise

SECRET   Copy 6
20th Machine Gun Coy - Wedges Orders

I. No 3 Section will take over at gun posns
   51, 52, 53, 54 by 1st No 2. M.G. Coy on 7th inst.

II. A guide from each gun team will be
    sent to M.G. Coy H.Q. by 4 P.M.

III. Tripods & belt boxes will be handed
     over in a clean state.

IV. Positions will be inspected by an
    officer before handing over, to
    ensure that guns are in a clean &
    sanitary condition.

V. Receipted list of French stores handed
   over to certificate that all gun posns
   were in a clean & sanitary condition
   will be rendered to RENK COY H.Q.
   on completion of relief.

VI. A limber will be at C.H. ST DRUCK
    at 5.45 p.m. for No 3 Section who
    will then proceed to RENK BILLETS.

VII. The relieving party on being relieved
     will proceed to RENK BILLETS under
     Capt Lawton

Renk Coy H.Q. 5.2.18   C Sailsby Lt
Copy 1 H.Q.   Commdg 20th M.G. Coy
     2 O.C. 2nd
     3 ""
     4 O.C. Bde
     5 ""
     6 ""
     7 file

SECRET Copy 4

204 Machine Gun Coy.
Relief Orders.

I. No 1 Section under 2 Lt W Smith will relieve guns of No 4 section at "B" Battery & 85 position on the 6th

II. All guns, spare parts boxes will be handed over with rest of material at positions.

III. Rations & water will be carried for 7th & 8th

IV. Relief will be completed by 5 pm and a report sent to ADV. COY. HQ. by No 1 Section

V. On completion of relief No 4 Section will proceed to REAR BILLETS

C. Saxby Lt.
Cmdg 204 M.G. Coy.

Rear Coy. HQ.
5.2.18
Copy 1 - OC
    2 - OC 1 Sect.
    3 - OC 4 -
    4 } - War Diary
    5 }
    6 - File

SECRET   Copy 6

204 Machine Gun Coy. Relief Orders

I. The 2 guns at B Battery will be relieved by 149 M.G. Coy on the afternoon of the 8th inst. – 85 position will be relieved by 245 M.G. Coy on the evening of the 8th inst.

II. Guides will be provided by M.G. Coy if called for.

III. Dugouts & gun pits will be handed over in a clean state.

IV. Positions will be inspected by an Officer before handing over to ensure that they are in a clean & sanitary condition.

V. A receipted list of Trench Stores handed over & a certificate that the positions were in a clean & sanitary condition will be given to REAR COY H.Q. on completion of relief.

VI. A limber will be at GASOMETER at 5.15 p.m. for guns of both Sections which will then proceed to REAR BILLETS.

Rear Coy H.Q. 5.2.18   C Saxby Lt.
Copy 1 to O.C.   Cmdg. 204 M.G. Coy
     2 – O.C. A Sec.
     3 – T.O.
     4 – 149 M.G.
     5,6 – Coy Diary
     7 –

SECRET.   204 MACHINE GUN COMPANY.   Copy No. 8

1. The 204 Machine Gun Coy. will proceed to new area by rail on the 17th inst.
   Entraining Station PROVEN
   The train will halt for 1 hour at TINQUES.

2. The Company will march from SCHOOL CAMP at 5.0 a.m. and the transport will be drawn up on the POPERINGHE ROAD at this time (a man with a light must be posted at the rear of the transport until daybreak)

3. Blankets, horse rugs and Officers valises must be by the motor lorry at 4.0 a.m.
   Blankets are to be rolled tightly by gun teams or in rolls of 10.
   A fatigue party of 20 men will report to the T.O. to carry horse rugs and blankets to the motor lorry.

4. Rations for 17th inst. (with the exception of breakfast ration) will be made in sections and distributed on the train. Tea and sugar will be kept in bulk and handed over to the cooks who will make tea at TINQUES.
   Rations for the 18th inst. will be carried by the train waggon which accompanies the Company to its destination.

5. 2/Lt. R.P. Shaw with 1 N.C.O. & 4 men will accompany the motor lorry to the entraining point. Special instructions will be issued later.

6. Nos 2 & 4 sections under 2/Lt. H. Kenchington will assist in entraining the horses and mules. Nos 1 & 3 sections under 2/Lt. R.P. Shaw will entrain the vehicles.

7. Each section will detail 3 brakesmen for their own limbers.

8. The attention of all men must be drawn to the train orders which forbid the doors of trucks to be opened while the train is travelling, Also empty bottles and other refuse being thrown on to the railway track, any man to leave the train at any time unless by the orders of an officer.

204 M.G. Coy. HQ.
14.2.18.

[signature] 2/Lt Adjt.
CAPTAIN
COMDG. NO. 204 M.G. COY.

Copies 1. C.O
       2. 2nd in Command
       3. T.O.
       4. O.C. No. 3 Section
       5. O.C. No. 4 "
       6. File
       7. War Diary
       8.

SECRET.   204 MACHINE GUN COMPANY.   Copy No. 8

Ref. Sheet 62c
 "   "   62D.

MOVE 1. The 204 M.G. Coy will move into the Cavalry Corps area as follows.
    (a) On Feb 24th by march, route from HARBONNIERES SUB AREA to staging camp about 1½ miles west of VILLERS CARBONNEL.
    (b) On Feb. 25th by march, route from VILLERS CARBONNEL to BERNES-HANCOURT AREA. (details to follow)
    (c) Orders to follow.

MARCH DETAILS 2. The Company will march out from present Billets at 9.40 a.m. on the 24th inst. & will join in the Brigade column at point R25 c 5.3. at 10.30. a.m.

BILLETING PARTIES 3. Lieut. C.V. Booth & 4 NCOs will proceed to the first staging area on bicycles leaving FRAMERVILLE at 9.0. a.m. & arrange for billets. This same party will proceed to the BERNES AREA on 25th inst.

CLEANLINESS OF BILLETS 4. All Billets must be left scrupulously clean. Tins & rubbish must be dumped in the authorised place. Section Officers will personally satisfy themselves on the above.

SMARTNESS OF TURN OUT AND MARCH DISCIPLINE 5. The Brigade will probably be inspected on the march by the G.O.C. Division. Every effort must be made to turn out clean and smart.
Particular attention must be paid to march discipline.
Singing on the march should be encouraged.

204 M.G. Coy.
H.Q.
               [signature]
               Adjutant.
               No. 204 Machine Gun Co.

Copies 1. C.C.
        2. 2nd in Command
        3. T.O.
        4. O.C. No 1 Sect
        5. "   2 "
        6. "   3 "
        7. "   4 "
        8,9) War Diary
        10 Spare

www.ingramcontent.com/pod-product-compliance
Lightning Source LLC
Chambersburg PA
CBHW081432160426
43193CB00013B/2263